Recharge Your Team

Recharge Your Team

The Grounded Visioning Approach

Jay W. Vogt

Westport, Connecticut
London

Library of Congress Cataloging-in-Publication Data

Vogt, Jay W.
    Recharge your team : the grounded visioning approach / by Jay W. Vogt.
        p. cm.
    Includes bibliographical references and index.
    ISBN 978–0–313–35542–4 (alk. paper)
    1. Employees—Coaching of. 2. Teams in the workplace—Management. 3. Employee
motivation. I. Title.
HF5549.5.C53V64 2009
658.4'022—dc22   2008033684

British Library Cataloguing in Publication Data is available.

Library of Congress Catalog Card Number: 2008033684
ISBN: 978–0–313–35542–4

First published in 2009

Praeger Publishers, 88 Post Road West, Westport, CT 06881
An imprint of Greenwood Publishing Group, Inc.
www.praeger.com

Printed in the United States of America

The paper used in this book complies with the
Permanent Paper Standard issued by the National
Information Standards Organization (Z39.48–1984).

10 9 8 7 6 5 4 3 2 1

To the stillness within us

Contents

Preface

When there is no vision, the people perish.

—Proverbs 29:18

If you work with people in organizations, this book is for you. However you connect with people—as an executive, consultant, group manager, volunteer, team member, project leader, technical expert, etc.—you care about results. And, to a great degree, you achieve those results through people.

So you're probably always looking for ways to help people accomplish as much as possible. This book describes a way to do that by helping all the members of your team gather together to create a shared vision for the future.

With a positive vision of the future, people in organizations excel. When people come together around common goals, they cooperate more easily, communicate better, give more of themselves, spark new ideas.

As a consultant, I see this again and again. With vision, organizational life is great. Without vision, it stinks. People are bored, unhappy, uninspired.

Most leaders understand this. They sense when the future appears hazy. They can see that their organization is losing direction. They observe that people seem tired. They realize that they have lost focus. Not a lot gets done, or what does get done feels like people are going through the motions.

In this situation, leaders know they must bring people together. The group needs to rediscover its shared vision. It's time to recharge. It's time for "strategic planning" or "brainstorming" or a "retreat." But the idea of an unstructured planning session with an uncertain end point can be daunting.

Often, leaders don't know where to start. People frequently hate the idea of a meeting, and it's easy for individuals at all levels to be cynical about yet another attempt to change the world. In fact, leaders can worry that getting together will make things worse. Most leaders know what they don't want: too much complaining, embarrassing sharing of personal feelings, setting of impossible goals followed by the inevitable letdown, endless talking that wastes time, no idea of what to do when the meeting is over.

In my decades of consulting experience, I have met many leaders faced with this challenge. Repeatedly, my clients have asked me to do what seemed impossible at the time: to bring together very diverse teams, organizations, and even whole communities in very short time frames (a half day or less) to discover a shared organizational vision for the future that, until then, had remained hidden to members of the organization.

Frankly, in earlier years, I lacked the process to pull this off. The groups I worked with needed lots of time to create a vision: typically two to four days. For clients, that meant lots of commitment and lots of money.

Eventually, however, I pioneered a new way of working that is both simple and powerful. I call it Grounded Visioning: "Grounded" because it builds upon the successes of the past and "Visioning" because it looks forward to an exciting future.

This method has proved effective for work teams, arts organizations, educational institutions, environmental advocacy groups, trade associations, and small businesses. It creates a shared vision that is fun, effective, and fast:

- **Fun.** People enjoy recalling the accomplishments of the past.
- **Effective.** People become energized to implement a shared vision of the future.
- **Fast.** Grounded Visioning takes a half day or less.

Recharge Your Team was inspired by the leaders who pushed me to create my own vision of Grounded Visioning. Recharged by their example, I present practical advice, checklists, and agendas that you can use to energize your own organization.

Acknowledgments

I thank my wife Stephanie and my daughter Camilla for their love and support. I thank my publishing coach Ken Lizotte of Emerson Consulting Group Inc. for helping me take my place as a thought leader and for helping me find my publisher.

I thank my editor Jeff Olson and Praeger Publishers for seeing how many organizations could be helped by these ideas.

I thank my local editor Claire Greene for helping me stretch toward my two goals for this manuscript: to get it done and to have it be good.

I thank my illustrator Cindy Murphy for her warm, effective illustrations and her upbeat, ever-steady support of my marketing efforts.

I thank Patricia L. Welch for bringing consistency to the endnotes.

I thank my colleagues who helped me experiment with and develop these ideas in the ever-hot crucible of live practice, particularly Denise Cormier, Erline Belton, and Ora Grodsky.

I thank the organizational development giants in my field who have taught me and inspired me in doing this work, particularly David Cooperrider, Diana Whitney, Marvin Weisbord, Sandra Janoff, Kathy Dannemiller, and Harrison Owen.

I thank my clients for the incredible privilege of allowing me to work with them at their growing edge. I thank them for being willing to take risks in trusting their people, in trying new things, and in allowing their futures to emerge from lively, unpredictable conversation. I thank them for their trust in this process and, ultimately, in themselves.

Finally, I give special thanks to consultant and author Bernard J. Mohr for the inspiration for this volume. He read the original article and first saw the book in it. He introduced me to publishers, helped frame the story, and contributed ideas. He was generous and encouraging with his support. He helped ignite my passion to make these tools and concepts available and helpful to a much larger audience of people and organizations. Thank you, Bernard.

PART I

Grounded Visions
Recharge Teams

Vision: The Foundation for Success

A team that has a shared vision has a reason to come to work every day.

I would give all the wealth of the world, and all the deeds of all the heroes, for one true vision.

—Henry David Thoreau

The most effective teams and organizations in the world have a shared sense of where they are going and what they aim to accomplish when they get there.

- Entrepreneurs see a need and aim to fill it.
- Retailers know what customers want and aspire to deliver it.
- Sports teams taste victory and do what it takes to win.
- Healers appreciate the synergy of whole body health.
- Community groups imagine a better future and the well being it brings.
- Educators envision their students' competency in action.

I call this having a shared vision of the future. When collaborators share a vision, they have a framework for making choices. People still disagree. Money is still scarce. Time is still short.

But with a shared vision, people can work within these constraints.

A team with a shared sense of direction is like a group of jazz musicians with a unifying musical theme. Each musician is free to go his or her way within the unifying choices made by the group. With every note, the musicians feel a greater sense of connection, as their joint efforts take them to a place they couldn't reach on their own. These musicians may be working hard, but they are definitely having fun. And the results are better because the musicians have the freedom to improvise when opportunities arise.

As with music, for community groups and businesses, a shared theme or vision is essential. Business literature and management advice books are full of the central importance of vision to an organization's success.

Jim Collins, author of the classic works *Good to Great* and *Built to Last,* says, "Vision is one of the least understood—yet most important—concepts for building great organizations."[1]

Author and management theorist Peter Senge defines vision as "the capacity to hold a shared picture of the future we seek to create." Senge writes, "When there is a genuine vision (as opposed to the all-too-familiar 'vision statement'), people excel and learn, not because they are told to, but because they want to."[2]

AN INSPIRING VIEW OF THE FUTURE

A vision for a community, organization, or team lays out a positive image of a future that inspires action in the present to make it real. It is a set of aspirations that represent the next great stretch for everyone committed to bring it about. It trumpets a resounding "absolutely yes!" to those actions that are consistent with its attainment and a resounding "absolutely no!" to those that are not.

Organizations that make time for a productive pause to find their vision discover—from their own people—what their dreams, hopes, and aspirations for the future really are.

- To a clean energy council, it is meeting or exceeding a set of ambitious metrics and targets for a robust regional clean energy economy.
- To a community college, it is being the key player in its community in meeting the needs of students and employers for twenty-first-century jobs.
- To a natural meats company, it is having its hot dog be the snack food of choice to America's children.
- To a small town, it is channeling all new growth and renovation in ways that are consistent with "smart growth" principles of appropriate density, mixed uses, and environmental sensitivity.
- To a team of medical clinician trainers, it is achieving new breakthroughs in operational efficiency, training that transforms behaviors, and research-based insights.
- To a small construction company, it is being a leader in green remodeling by building competency and passion as an employee-managed company.

These organizations enjoy a competitive advantage in the marketplace because their clear articulation of a preferred future:

- Engages more of the whole person within each organization by connecting with their passion and emotion.
- Focuses effort by giving people a reason to say yes to certain activities and no to others.
- Gives people a clear outcome at which to aim, enabling them to better seize opportunities that present themselves and more skillfully improvise as needed to overcome obstacles with a clear end in mind.

WHAT MAKES AN EFFECTIVE VISION?

A compelling and believable vision has three components:[3]

- **Continuity.** When visions carry forward the best of the past, they ensure that the past and people's contributions to it are valued—thus allowing people to experience an essential sense of continuity and worth as they create anew.
- **Innovation.** When visions incorporate images of new results and ways of being, they introduce the essential element of innovation.
- **Transition.** When visions include suggestions and implications for how we will create the future, people begin to see the probability that the transition from here to there is possible.

Continuity

An effective vision must carry forward the best of the past. What has worked in the past is a tremendous resource for success in the future. That resource must be accessed and celebrated. Most of the same people who created the organization's past are likely to be the ones creating its future. They need to know that their contributions are valued. A focus on how the organization works when it is at its very best creates a foundation of possibility and pride on which an innovative future can be imagined and achieved.

For example, a team specializes in improving the performance of clinical teams through challenging medical simulation experiences. Team members noted these strengths in their Grounded Visioning session:

- "We operate well under pressure and enjoy working on the edge."
- "Everyone feels that other members of the team can be the go-to person that picks up just where they are needed."

That is something any team would want to keep!

Innovation

An effective vision must be innovative. It must extend the old into the new. It must offer a challenge worthy of the best efforts of those who will create it. It must stimulate and inspire. It must challenge and perhaps even provoke. Ultimately, it must connect with and express the dreams, hopes, and aspirations of the people who make up the team, organization, or community.

For example, with the simulation training team, its passion for innovation in the future was to prove to the widest possible audience, through stellar research, how powerful this work was in improving patient safety through the higher functioning of clinical teams.

Transition

An effective vision must be achievable. People must be invited to help map out the path to its attainment. They must be engaged not only in its creation but also in its implementation. They must be stretched by its innovation and comforted by its feasibility. A vision that builds on the past, extends into the future, and suggests a bridge to that future is a complete and compelling vision.

For our simulation trainers, this meant investing in new staff positions to support expanded research and to develop new products that would keep them at the cutting edge.

WHEN IS IT TIME FOR A VISION SESSION?

In today's complex world, every organization or team enters a phase now and then when its future appears hazy. People lose focus about their direction. You hear people say, "We lack a shared vision" and "We don't know where we are going." There is more grumbling, needless conflict, and wasted effort than before. Energy is low, and frustration is high. People want to contribute, but they are not sure how. They sense that something is missing, but they're not even sure what.

These may be the symptoms of an organization that is working just fine but not working *toward* something. They may be the danger signs of an organization that is going through the motions but not moving toward a shared goal. They could be expressions of a group that is taking care of business in the present but not building toward the future. These signs are saying that it is time for a vision session.

A team that has a shared vision has a reason to come to work every day. Team members see how what they are doing on Monday morning relates to where they want to be at the end of the year. They can seize on opportunities and work around obstacles to keep moving toward their goal. They can tell a friend at a party not only what they do for a living but also what they are creating by doing it. These signs are saying that the vision is alive and well.

Many leaders who stay in tune with their people can tell the difference. They can sense their people's doubts and concerns about the lack of a shared vision. They know they should do something about it, but they're not sure what. They feel they should bring their people together, but they're not sure how.

TODAY'S VISIONS ARE COLLABORATIVE

How does your organization go about creating its vision? Through the ages, visions were a religious experience. Solitary. Revelatory. The supernatural spoke; saints and prophets listened and passed on the vision to their followers. Followers followed.

Today's business world is collaborative. One day, a person may be a leader. The next day, he or she is a follower. Lines of authority may not be clear. People frequently must inspire the voluntary cooperation of others whom they do not supervise.

That's why visions can't be "handed down" anymore. Dictates from on high don't inspire people to work together, to go beyond what's expected of them, to imagine. To work hard "not because they are told to, but because they want to," as Senge puts it.

That means your vision must reflect the thinking of many different people. For example, a community music school would want to involve all the following in its planning: its own teachers, public school educators, local musicians, parents, neighbors, other performing artists, donors, students, local officials, state arts administrators.

To tap the thinking of all these constituencies, you're going to need a meeting. You could speak with people separately, but there will be nagging doubts that some constituency is more equal than others. And you'll lose out on the creative imagining that occurs when people with different perspectives share ideas in real time.

MEETINGS WE LOVE TO HATE

But don't worry. Your meeting doesn't have to be long or boring or contentious. It needn't be expensive. It doesn't have to be the kind of meeting my clients love to hate:

- A "blue-sky" session, where anything goes, that leaves the team feeling less connected to reality than they were before. We know managers who have been talked into sessions like this and tolerated them, only to clamp down afterward tighter than before, bringing everyone "back to basics."
- A "touchy-feely" session, where people feel embarrassed or awkward. Paint ball. Karaoke. The cartoon series, "Dilbert," and the television series, "The Office," have brought these in-house, organizational clichés to a national audience. The saddest part is that most people desperately want to feel something for their work, they just hate touchy-feely.
- An expensive session, where high-priced consultants run up an exorbitant bill. We all know consultants are expensive. When you bill by the hour, don't you naturally want a longer meeting?
- A gripe session, where everyone comes together and moans and leaves feeling worse than before. These meetings are as tragic as train-wrecks because nobody wants them, but once on course, they can't be stopped.
- A top-down session, where people come away without feeling any buy-in or commitment. This type of meeting can feel like the most efficient course when the leader sits down to map out his or her vision. What leaders forget is that delay and resistance come when people are asked to implement something they had no part in creating.
- A long session that takes people away from their jobs for days at a time. Time is money, and resources are short. Clients are always asking us to do more in less time.

Do these sound like some of the meetings you never want to have?

If so, you're not alone.

In my consulting practice, I hear this time after time. Leaders know they need vision. Leaders know they have to bring diverse personalities together to create vision. Leaders worry that the progress of the meeting itself will derail the vision. It will take too long and people will get bored. It will never happen because it

---

Why Do Organizations Lack Vision?

- **Vision:** A shared sense of direction as to where an organization is going and what it aims to accomplish when it gets there.
- **The need:** Stakeholders need a shared vision in order to collaborate effectively.
- **The problem:** Most attempts to define a vision take too long, cost too much, and don't get results.

---

could be too expensive. There won't be follow-through because everyone doesn't feel as if his or her opinions and ideas had equal weight.

These are all very real dangers. But it is possible to make a vision session that is the very opposite of these clichés.

WHAT MAKES A VISION SESSION WORK?

Leaders have shared with me what they seek in a visioning meeting. They want sessions that are:

- **Practical.** The vision that emerges must be bold enough to inspire, yet practical enough to feel achievable.
- **Pragmatic.** Leaders want visioning that is grounded in the successes of the past and the realities of the present.
- **Inexpensive.** Visioning can't tie up expensive personnel and consultants for days.
- **Positive.** The session must tap the natural excitement and enthusiasm for a positive future that is present in everyone.
- **Collaborative.** For a vision to have staying power, it must be shared. People support what they help create. For people to support a new vision, they must be involved in creating it. Results must be widely owned.
- **Fast.** Let's be done in four hours or less. Two would be better.

This is the challenge presented by my clients, and Grounded Visioning is my response.

An inspiring vision of the future that is grounded in the best of the past is a "Grounded Vision." The process starts with identifying the things that have given us life in the past and that we want to carry into the future.

This is why I call this process "Grounded" visioning. It is the best of the future grounded on the best of the past. When this happens, we have created a vision of immeasurable value.

NOTES

1. Jim Collins in "Building Your Company's Vision" at http://www.jimcollins.com/lab/buildingVision/ (accessed May 27, 2008).

2. Peter M. Senge, *The Fifth Discipline. The Art & Practice of the Learning Organization* (London: Random House, 1990), 9.

3. S. Srivastva and R.E. Fry, eds., *Executive and Organizational Continuity: Managing the Paradoxes of Stability and Change* (San Francisco: Jossey-Bass, 1992).

2

Six Steps to Your Organization's Vision

Focus on what's good about your team to create an achievable vision.

[W]e'll look, not at visions, but at realities.
—Edith Wharton, *The Age of Innocence*

Grounded Visioning is my response to the planning challenges faced by many organizations. Not much time. Not much money. Lots of stakeholders. Lots at stake.

I have used this method successfully with boards and managements of nonprofit organizations, with teams in large corporations, with interested members of a community, with the boards or management of new and evolving businesses, and with government agencies. Grounded Visioning works with these different types of groups because it focuses on generating visionary ideas that are "grounded" in past achievements. It's fast. It's fun. It recharges organizations.

In later chapters, I will explain how this process works in detail. I will show you how you can customize this protocol to your unique needs. This chapter presents an overview of the basic method and highlights the steps using the case of the Arts and Crafts Guild.[1]

The Arts and Crafts Guild is a venerable big-city institution, more than 100 years old. The Guild approached me some time ago to create a shared vision for the organization. It wanted to involve three groups that had never worked together before: the Board of Trustees, the Resource Council, and the Advisory Council. Like many clients, the Guild felt an urgent need, yet could commit little time—just one evening, in fact. So much need, so little time!

Using the process outlined here, I enabled these three stakeholder groups to discover their shared vision in about three hours.

In just three hours, you, too, can accomplish these six steps:

- Assemble your stakeholders
- Ignite your spark
- Share best practices
- Share your dreams
- Select the best
- Plan next steps

ASSEMBLE YOUR STAKEHOLDERS

Start by bringing together everyone who has a stake in the future of your organization. Generally speaking, stakeholders may be people who are informed about the task at hand, who will be affected by the task at hand, or who can influence it in some way. With a business that could mean employees, union representatives, and managers, but it could also mean suppliers and customers. With a college that certainly means faculty, staff, and administrators, but typically also includes students, alumni, community leaders, educators, and business people. A small group session could very profitably consist only of a single team that can sit around one table. Or it could include several other teams with whom that one team interacts and their management in a large group meeting.

In the case of the Arts and Crafts Guild, key staff members came together with three groups composed of crafts artisans and business people: the Board of Trustees, the Resource Council, and the Advisory Council. These

Figure 2.1

Six steps to a Grounded Vision: Assemble your stakeholders. Ignite your spark. Share best practices. Share your dreams. Select the best. Plan next steps.

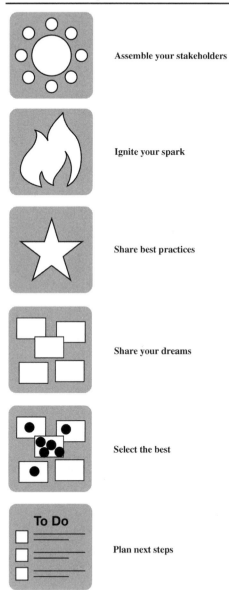

Assemble your stakeholders

Ignite your spark

Share best practices

Share your dreams

Select the best

Plan next steps

Illustration by Cindy Murphy.

stakeholders had never met and worked together before, and between them they comprised about 40 people. The Board had overall responsibility for the governance of the organization. The Resource Council helped provide access to needed institutional resources. The Advisory Council gave guidance on thinking related to the evolving world of contemporary craft.

Forty people were far too many people to fit around a table, so we needed to break this larger group up into a series of smaller groups. Typically that means breaking a large group of 40 into five groups of 8 and challenging each group to do some of the visioning work themselves, with the session moderator's guidance and direction.

Other than a few key staff members, participants were volunteers who most likely held full-time jobs elsewhere. So the meeting was held in the evening, at the Guild space downtown, on a weekday at six. Dinner was ready as people arrived, and the real work began promptly at 6:30 P.M.

IGNITE YOUR SPARK

Every visioning process needs a spark that ignites people's passion for what is possible. Visioning involves creating a picture of something that doesn't now exist yet has the capacity to move you into action. As Rosabeth Moss Kanter says, "A vision is not just a picture of what could be; it is an appeal to our better selves, a call to become something more."[2] That sounds like a perfect job for the right brain, the hemisphere that works in images, possibilities, and intuition. The more linear left brain, the hemisphere that works in logic, analysis, and words, will have its moment to excel in evaluating the opportunities that the right brain creates and in mapping out their implementation. But to have that material to work with, the visioning process needs to tap people's innate creativity, intuition, and emotion.

For our quick spark, we ask participants to interview each other in a decidedly positive way. People find a partner (preferably someone they don't know), ask the partner four questions, and write down the answers.

- **Attractions.** What attracted you to this organization and keeps you committed?
- **High points.** Tell a story about a time when you felt most connected with, committed to, and proud of this organization.
- **Dreams.** Name three dreams, hopes, and aspirations you have for what you want this organization to be or do.
- **Optimism.** Name one reason for optimism that these dreams can come true.

As you can see, these interview questions assume a strong positive bias. Because they involve appreciating what you have, they are called "appreciative interviews," a term that will be used throughout this book. We all know there are low points in organizations, but for now, we are not interested. Our intention is to tap the wellspring of positive emotion for the organization and to ground our visioning in how the organization is when it is at its very best. Having done that, we want to dare our participants to share their dreams, hopes, and aspirations. Finally, we ask them to convince themselves, with reasons for optimism, that these dreams could actually come true. We are sparking something visionary and extraordinary, and we don't want to be timid.

Back at the Guild, people have their instructions and are starting to chat. Participants are seated at tables in assigned seats so that Board members are mixed with Resource Council and Advisory Council members. Thus, interview pairs are connecting people from different parts of the organization who might not otherwise interact. These interviews double as icebreaking relationship builders, so that by the time they are done, people are feeling more relaxed and connected. The energy in the room is moving, and you can sense greater excitement and curiosity.

SHARE BEST PRACTICES

We ask people to call out what attracted them to this organization and what keeps them involved. This short exercise reawakens everyone's commitment to the organization. It reminds them of why they got involved in the first place. It reveals their personal connection and that of those around them. It maps the vital core of what motivates inspired team players.

Some of the replies at the Arts and Crafts Guild included:

- Being part of an historical movement—the oldest arts and crafts organization in the country.
- Having a positive impact on the craft community.
- Unique opportunity to be involved with a diverse mix of people and artists.
- Positive attitude of the people involved.

We ask people to share a few stories that they especially liked hearing—or telling— about times where they felt most engaged and committed to the organization. One Guild participant recalled creating a craft guide; the experience of going from nothing to something transformed her personally, was useful to the craft community, and pulled her into the Guild as a volunteer for good. Another recalled working on the marketing committee, the dedication of this small working group, and how they realized they could be anything they wanted to be and so began to dream and achieve even bigger!

After hearing a few of these stories, common themes naturally emerge. Often I will headline a blank poster with this sentence as a prompt, "When we are at our best, we...," and ask the group to complete it. That is usually enough to draw a variety of responses. Sometimes I offer up a theme that has emerged. Together these themes describe the organization at its very best.

Participants at the Arts and Crafts Guild said that, when we are at our best, we...

- Roll up our sleeves on behalf of the organization in a satisfying, fulfilling way.
- Spark small group action that leads to significant accomplishment.

- Create sharing between patrons, artists, and the public.
- Lead and serve as pioneers in creativity, art, and craft.
- Enjoy endless opportunities to learn something new.

SHARE YOUR DREAMS

At this point, still early in the process, the energy in the room has already shifted dramatically. People are engaged, proud, and relaxed. Sharing key attractors reawakens commitment. Sharing high points releases extraordinary amounts of positive energy and affection for the one thing everyone in the room has in common—the organization and its mission. Now we are ready to share our dreams of the future with each other.

We ask each individual to write his or her three dreams for the future on three sticky notes (one per note), come to the front of the room, and read them aloud. By this simple action, everyone takes responsibility for contributing his or her hopes for the future. Before people sit down, we ask them to post their notes on large sheets of butcher paper. The first person has the easiest job—he or she can post anywhere. After that, people have to decide whether or not their idea echoes an existing one, and, if so, they physically place it nearby. And so, step-by-step, with little or no consultant intervention, a shared vision, created by physical clusters of like ideas, begins to emerge. This clustering is called "affinity diagramming," a term you will see throughout this book. Watching from the audience is like seeing a photograph emerge from its chemical bath. Fuzzy at first, it becomes clearer and clearer with time. It is exciting to watch.

After all the dreams are posted, we review them briefly and make sure they're all in the right places. This means walking back through and reading as many as 120 notes (for a group of 40 working together). If that is too much information to process, you can divide the large group into groups of 8 that do some of the synthesizing work at their tables before sharing it with everyone else.

For every cluster we find, we ask the group for a name that summarizes the essence of the shared idea and add it as a header. If there is any confusion about where a note belongs, we defer to the author. What emerges from all those individual data points is a set of shared, common aspirations.

After sorting sticky notes with the Guild, 17 themes emerged, among them:

- Secure appropriate facility.
- Network more between crafts organizations.
- Build the brand.
- Support emerging artists.
- Educate the public.

SELECT THE BEST

It is hard to help large, diverse groups reach consensus quickly. To get results fast, we must cut corners just a bit. We take a shortcut called "multi-voting." In multi-voting each participant gets an equal number of votes. We distribute an equal supply of adhesive dots to everyone. A common rule of thumb is to give a number of dots equal to one-third of the number of total options. The Guild staff and volunteers, choosing among 17 options, got six dots (or votes) each. This is not so much decision-making as preference sharing.

I ask everyone, while still in his or her seat, to choose which themes in the emerging shared vision seem most compelling and most promising. Then I have everyone come up and vote by placing the dots—everyone at once so as not to influence each other. In a few minutes, the voting is over.

At the Guild, the most votes went to two visions:

- Secure appropriate facility.
- Achieve financial security.

The voting revealed a second tier of dreams:

- Educate the public.
- Support emerging artists.
- Support artists.
- Host craft show.
- Build brand.

As you can see from this example, this straw poll shows you what is most popular but not whether or not there is a consensus. But often the results of the vote are vivid enough to quickly lead to consensus. So you start with multi-voting and then test for consensus and see what happens.

In the Guild's case, two results jumped off the walls. The idea, tossed about for years, that the Guild should be a museum died—on the spot. It had been dutifully proposed and yet there were almost no votes for it. Everyone had, independently, concluded that the idea no longer held merit. And so—in an instant—the organization was finally able to say, "No," to a long-debated strategic direction.

At the same time, the votes revealed that many people held a private hope that the organization would one day convene a major crafts fair to raise money, support artists, and build brand. This had in fact been the means by which the organization's founders came together more than a century before, but the idea had long since been dormant. No one really believed others shared this bold vision. When it became apparent that many in the room actually did, the enthusiasm for it was immediate and palpable.

PLAN NEXT STEPS

Imagine that you have now done what might have seemed impossible only a couple hours before. You have brought together a large, diverse group of people who have never worked together and helped them find an exciting common

The Language of Grounded Visioning

- **Appreciative interviews:** Appreciative interviews are a quick, interactive way for individuals to discover (or "appreciate") what works about a team or organization. The questions in the interview process have an unabashedly strong positive bias to help quickly discover strengths, assets, and sources of vitality.
- **Affinity diagramming:** Affinity diagramming is a quick, visual way to find (or "diagram") common themes (or "affinities") among lots of individual data points. After each point of data is posted separately on an adhesive note, it is easy to physically cluster them together, like with like, to discover common themes.
- **Multi-voting:** Multi-voting is a quick, visual way to express and record preferences of members of a group. Individual members get multiple adhesive dots to cast as votes among their top preferences. After everyone takes a quick trip from chair to wall to place their dots, the group's top preferences become instantly visible.

ground that none had previously recognized. There is great excitement and a sense of possibility in the room. Your time together is almost spent, but there is one more important thing to do.

The final act in a Grounded Visioning session is to map out next steps. Often there is not enough time for action planning of any consequence. More likely, you or some other leader will ask for volunteers to meet and plan next steps in the top areas of interest. Because so many people have participated in creating the vision, there is usually no shortage of people who want to help make it happen.

The best time to plan likely next steps is before the event, while planning the meeting. Imagine that clear top priorities do emerge. Imagine that committed volunteers do step forward. How do you want to manage your success? There are lots of good strategies for following through. The key is to pick ones that fit with the culture of your team, organization, or community and to be ready to implement them.

Back at the Guild, we're running out of time, so we ask for volunteers to explore top priority items at a future date, perhaps in teams. Given more time, we might ask interested parties, right then, to form working groups around top priority goals and to create action plans on the spot.

You'll remember that we ask four questions in our "quick spark" interviews. What do we do with the answers to the fourth—our reasons for optimism? In our last few minutes together, with the excitement and anxiety of big dreams still fresh in the air, we end the meeting by asking people to call out their reasons for believing their compelling shared vision can actually come to pass. These reasons for optimism are a final affirmation that the vision is grounded in reality and a means of identifying practical ideas, resources, and assets that can be used to bring the dream to reality.

At the Guild, a working group of staff and volunteers eagerly embraced the idea of a crafts fair. The group quickly researched the best similar events around the country, built an exhibition planning model based on the best practices, and put it in motion. The standard time for organizing a first exhibition was 18 months, but this group pulled off the first show in 9. Reasons for optimism, indeed.

Less than one year later, the Guild premiered Craft City, a four-day, juried show of 145 studio artists featuring one-of-a-kind and limited-edition pieces in basketry, ceramics, fiber, glass, jewelry, leather, metal, paper, wood, and other media that was seen by 5,000 people. The show not only broke even but also returned a substantial profit. The following year, Craft City attracted 160 artists and even more visitors, and in the third year 175 artists and yet more visitors. Craft City has since become a core program that is fundamental to the Guild's success.

Craft City realized many of the stakeholders' hopes through a stunning synergy:

- **Building brand** by becoming recognized as "the leading show and exhibition of fine contemporary craft in New England" and "one of the top craft shows in the United States."
- **Supporting artists and emerging artists** through enhanced opportunities for hundreds of artists to show and sell their work, earning up to $55,000 per artist per show.
- **Achieving greater financial security** by contributing, in 2004, 43 percent of the Guild's budget and a six-figure net contribution. In fact, added their executive director, "Craft City saved us through the recent economic downturn."
- **Educating the public** through lectures, tours, and other educational programs.

"This idea is very mission compatible," concluded their executive director. "It's a complete match with who we are." And it emerged in three and a half hours, including dinner and a break.

NOTE

1. Every case in this book features a real organization but uses a fictional name.
2. http://www.brainyquote.com/quotes/authors/r/rosabeth_moss_kanter.html (accessed May 27, 2008).

3

Why Grounded Visioning Works

Use a simple planning method that everyone can understand.

My interest is in the future, as I'm going to be spending the rest of my life there.
—Charles Kettering

Five attributes set Grounded Visioning apart from other visioning processes. Grounded Visioning is:

- **Fast,** meaning it can be completed in four hours or less, even with very large groups.
- **Grounded** in how the organization is when it is at its very best.
- **Visionary,** rather than merely incremental, in its view of the future.
- **Visual,** making it attractive to our fast-paced, highly visual culture.
- **Energizing,** since it resolves the tension between honoring the past and reinventing the future.

Let's examine each of these five attributes in greater detail. We'll use the case of a community conversation about kids and learning in a divided public school district to help make our points. Many feel that public schools represent the weaving that holds the civic fabric of democracy together. A public school system is designed to meet the needs of a local community while integrating that community into the larger and greater good of the whole society. Conflict between federal and local priorities and between the priorities of different segments of a diverse community is inevitable. What shape must visioning take in this context?

FAST: FOUR HOURS TO A SHARED VIEW OF THE FUTURE

Grounded Visioning is designed for speed. My clients are always asking me to do more with less. Nonprofit clients feel the pressure of greater competition for diminished donor attention and dollars. State agencies feel the burden of serving a public with increasing expectations for services and a decreasing appetite for taxes. Companies feel the urgency of their ever-present reality of disruptive technological change and competitive attack. Leaders of all these organizations need a faster way to get their people focused and then get them refocused, again and again.

Organizations typically employ Grounded Visioning when they have four hours or fewer, even when they are bringing together very large groups. Grounded Visioning helps even large groups create shared visions quickly because it strips the visioning process down to its bare essentials:

- A simple, engaging process (paired appreciative interviews) that simultaneously honors the past, energizes the present, and illuminates the preferred future in a powerful and efficient way.
- A simple, engaging process (posting dreams in affinity diagrams) that integrates the discrete aspirations of multiple individuals into a collective, emerging aggregate set of aspirations in a powerful and efficient way.
- A simple, engaging process (multi-voting) that integrates the discrete preferences of multiple individuals into a collective, emergent set of priorities in a powerful and efficient way.

A team working in pairs can connect with the energizing essence at the core of the interviewing process in as little as 10 minutes. A team can further harvest the data that pour forth from that process in just half an hour. This same team can easily aggregate the insights about the future into a clear picture of a shared future in another hour or so. And it takes only 5 or 10 minutes to set priorities using multi-voting. Thus a team can go from a standstill to a finished product in as little as two hours.

The beauty of this speed is not only that organizations save time and money. Being fast also means that the activity of visioning comes off its pedestal and becomes a practice that teams can turn to readily, on an as-needed basis. We don't want the people in any organization to feel that they don't have enough time to envision their future.

Traditional Planning Takes Days

That may be the case for many organizations that are used to the standards set by the consulting profession. For many consultants, the gold standard in visioning experiences is the Future Search Conference designed by Marv Weisbord and Sandra Janoff.[1] It is an integrated set of experiences that builds community and envisions a preferred future, typically involving 64 people over two and one-half days. The first half-day breaks the ice and warms people to their task, asks them to recall significant events in the history of the organization and to reflect on what they mean, and maps out trends in the marketplace and the world outside that are shaping the organization. The second full day explores the implications of those trends, allowing stakeholders to share what in the present situation makes them proud and sorry, and then launches the community into a visioning activity involving hilarious skits, before finally finding common ground. The final day confirms the common ground and maps out action steps.

I have led Future Search Conferences and love them. Still, not many organizations have the time, money, and commitment to invest two and one-half days in these conversations, important though they may be.

Another powerful technique, the Appreciative Inquiry Summit, goes beyond the Future Search Conference to introduce new, even more powerful experiences to help participants create the future they want.[2] This is a powerful method but requires even more time—four days.

The first day is devoted to discovery of the organization's "positive core" through extended appreciative interviews and sharing. The second day is given to dreaming the organization's preferred, positive future. The third day is dedicated to designing a reinvented organization that can better live out its values and dreams. The fourth and final day is committed to destiny—the mapping of key initiatives by innovation teams charged with making it happen.

These visioning experiences are wonderful, but if you don't have the time and still want the essential result, Grounded Visioning is the method of choice.

Small Time Commitment Draws in Lots of Stakeholders

Let's see what fast means to a public school district with a very pressing dilemma and very little time in which to resolve it. A talented educator took a new job as the superintendent of the public schools in a working class New England mill town. He wanted a mandate to push for positive change. But this town had a history of voting down property tax overrides that would fund school operations above a bare-bones budget. Young parents lobbied hard for improvements; seniors living on fixed incomes begged for relief.

No vision, however brilliant, could be conceived and imposed on this passionately divided community. One segment or another would promptly reject and resist it. A shared visioning process would have to bring together diverse stakeholders who didn't particularly want to work together. The vision would have to emerge from the community, so the community—as a whole—would own it and commit to making it real. Given the short attention span of most community volunteers, this all had to happen quickly.

A call went out for community volunteers to participate in planning a community conversation about the town's kids and their learning. A deliberate effort was made to balance pro-school and antitax advocates. Despite their differences, this planning group quickly agreed on three things:

- The focus of any conversation would be about our kids and their learning, not budgets and overrides, and should build bridges and honor the diversity of views in town.
- Anyone who wanted to participate would be welcome, even if that meant accommodating hundreds of people.

- The community could not be expected to come together for any more than four hours. That was the limit. Four hours from start to finish, to find a common vision, among hundreds of people, in a divided community, is *fast*.

GROUNDED: BUILD ON SUCCESSES FROM YOUR PAST

Grounded Visioning begins with stories about high points in the organization's past. The paired interview process proactively seeks examples, stories, and cases that show the people of the organization functioning at their best. Like a mini-research project, it searches out best practices.

These stories reveal:

- **Capabilities**—like the ability to change lives—that are demonstrated by repeated achievements over time.
- **Strengths**—like tenacity in the face of obstacles—that are highlighted by proud successes.
- **Values**—like integrity in a world of compromise—that are cherished by those who see them put into practice.
- **Life-giving forces**—like a workplace community of appreciation, challenge, and fun—that nurture people as they work for the good of the organization.

These stories typically reveal themes with a high degree of consistency. That's because every organization has a unique culture, expressing both its strengths and its weaknesses, and stories are a uniquely efficient way to access it. They quickly take us to the heart of the organization, its very DNA. They show us what makes it tick and what makes it come alive.

People sharing these stories become animated, laugh, and get excited. It's like they uncap some kind of organizational artesian well, and the energy of the organization at its best comes bubbling up without effort. They connect with the reasons they care about the organization and what makes them come to work in the morning. A room full of people sharing these stories is fun and alive.

These stories show what people in the organization can do when they are at their very best; they ground dreams in reality. They increase the organization's awareness of its internal resources and capabilities. Yes, we all know that we are not at our best every day, but we forget how often we actually are at our best and how wonderful it feels. These stories remind us, and they give us hope. They provide the platform to imagine that the future we really want is one that we can truly attain. They generate an emotional field that supports a positive vision of the future. They give us permission to dream and the knowledge that we can make that dream a reality.

Community Members Share Stories about Their Town's Schools

Let's revisit our public school district. The diverse planning group settled on a Saturday morning in the spring and invited literally everyone in the community to come. Organizers spoke to community and business groups all over town, saying,

"We want consensus. We want diversity. We want action. We want you!" Parents organized enough offerings of food to host a lunch for all comers. Young people played music while participants gathered. That morning, organizers anxiously waited to see who, and how many, would come.

More than 130 people marched in and sat down at round tables of 8. (The town's population is around 10,000, so this was better than a one percent response rate—excellent for a survey response, let alone an in-person meeting.) They were seniors, educators, business leaders, students, alumni, town officials, K-12 parents, preschool parents, community leaders, and taxpayers. To ensure diverse conversations, volunteers at the registration table assigned folks randomly to table groups. Participants received a note explaining the reason for the assigned seating and requesting their cooperation.

After a welcome by the superintendent, we set in motion a round of appreciative storytelling at the tables—featuring in this case high points in the participants' experience of kids and learning in their town. The room was soon vibrant and alive with animated conversation. The stories provided a foundation of understanding in how people in this community learn when they are at their best. Seniors remembered their joy of learning as children. Adults and parents recounted their excitement at seeing the spark of learning in a son, daughter, young relative, or neighbor. Employers spoke of their satisfaction in hiring well-educated employees. Young people talked about the power of a mentor. After hearing the stories, the work groups at the tables were asked to list the common themes, and then develop one or two belief statements based on those themes. They were asked to complete the statement, "Our kids learn best when..." Some said:

- When the whole community supports them.
- When the right resources and tools are available.
- When a person who cares makes a difference.

We asked to hear a few stories as highlights, and they quickly surfaced moving testimony on the power of learning. The stage was set.

VISIONARY: IMAGINE THE BEST POSSIBLE FUTURE

Grounded Visioning asks its participants to dream, to hope, to aspire, and to imagine a positive future. But it grounds that future in how the organization is when it is at its very best. This approach feels at once both wise and exciting.

Much of the excitement generated by the process comes from the freedom it gives participants to imagine a positive future as they would want it to be. The implicit invitation is to answer the more radical internal question—what is it that I truly want for this organization?—rather than the seemingly more prudent question—what is it that I think we can get?

There is tremendous power and energy in connecting with what we really want. A room full of people sharing what they really want feels vital and alive.

Too Much Caution, Too Narrow a Vision

This freedom to imagine is not necessarily part of every strategic planning process. Classical strategic planning advises a more cautious approach, driven by an assessment of the current situation. Planners typically assess the Strengths and Weaknesses of the organization and the Opportunities and Threats in its environment (a SWOT analysis). This map of the organization's current reality and environment is used to create goals in a prudent, incremental way. Goals can be proposed, for example, to improve the organization's existing strengths and to minimize its existing weaknesses. Goals can be proposed to capitalize on the environment's existing opportunities and to neutralize its existing threats.

The SWOT approach is prudent and effective to a point. Yet it has a significant limitation. The process of creating goals in response to the organization's current reality locks that organization into incremental improvement. There is no inspiration to imagine dramatic change. This process, under the cloak of responsibility, assumes a significant risk. Planning based on current reality neglects to ask organizational participants about what they truly want, independent of existing conditions. Within such limits, it may be impossible to elicit innovative or even revolutionary aspirations.

Of course, it is risky to focus on what you truly want, rather than just on what seems possible. But such blue-sky thinking can be exhilarating. It is how most great innovation occurs. Someone, or some group, makes a discontinuous break with the past and a revolutionary, rather than just evolutionary, leap into the future.

Because Grounded Visioning is designed to take four hours or less, it cannot both look for incremental improvements and imagine a perfect future. In that short amount of time, people cannot both prudently review and respond to the organization's existing situation and envision what they truly want. So Grounded Visioning focuses on bringing out the energy and power of the visionary approach.

People Write Down Dreams for Their Schools

Let's return to our small town school district. The whole room was ready for a break after sharing stories and beliefs about learning. Now, 90 minutes into their morning, the citizens are back. We asked them to work in pairs, interviewing each other about two dreams, outcomes, or aspirations they have for their kids and their learning in the years ahead. We asked them to focus on what they truly want, not on how they can get it. We used our grounding in how the community learns when it is at its very best as the platform to leap into their desired future, with no further assessment or warm-up.

The individuals talked privately in pairs. They wrote their goals on simple adhesive notes. After just a few minutes, they returned their focus to their tables and worked with the other three pairs to report, post, and sort their aspirations. Speaking in pairs helps make it safe for introverted individuals to express their ideas. Within just a few minutes, every individual in the room of 130 had shared his or her fondest hopes for the future and written them down. The elements of a shared vision were in play.

VISUAL: SHOW ALL IDEAS TO INSPIRE COLLABORATION

Wonderful, heartwarming conversations are not enough to create powerful, shared visions. Peter Senge, reflecting on the challenge of creating shared vision, writes, "What has been lacking is a discipline for translating vision into shared vision—not a 'cookbook' but a set of principles and guiding practices. The practice of shared vision involves the skills of unearthing shared 'pictures of the future' that foster genuine commitment and enrolment rather than compliance."[3]

Interviews with an unabashed bias toward the positive are a great way to unearth shared "pictures of the future" in vivid words and phrases. The dreams, hopes, and aspirations that surface can be captured in brief words and phrases that can be written on sticky notes. These notes can be physically posted for all to see. Once posted, they can be clustered in similar groups. Once clustered, they can be titled with a header that captures the essence of the entire group of ideas.

This highly visual diagramming process creates vivid imagery in the minds of participants. First there is the physical picture that emerges from all of the individual data points, clustered together in like categories, with an overarching category header. A number of individual inputs that would otherwise easily be overwhelming becomes manageable by seeking and finding similar themes and representing those themes in a physical and spatial way.

Next there is a kind of metaphysical picture of the future that begins to form in the minds of participants. The many disparate individual data points, all originally shared individually by members of the team, organization, or community, come together in ways that reveal common views. This repetition of ideas begins to reveal some of the common ground that had previously been invisible to most participants. This sense of shared understanding, physically expressed by lots of data points coming from many different corners of the room—and now clustered together on the wall—helps participants form a mental image of an emerging common ground.

Visual Presentation Makes Everyone a Decision Maker

This highly visual experience is both transparent and definitive. The process is transparent because data from every participant are shared publicly. Everyone can see every idea. No group of planners is more equal than others. Everyone has access to the same information. Everyone can see how ideas are sorted—the people "in charge" are not manipulating suggestions. The emergence of themes feels like a simple, leaderless process, where the will of the people is not imposed, but revealed.

The transparency of the process means that people feel good that their ideas are taken seriously. This is no suggestion box where ideas go in but don't come out. Here, people can literally see their ideas being used. They can see that their ideas are important and needed and that they contributed to the outcome. If their views don't carry the day, they at least got heard and seen. There is a clear incentive to make a high-quality contribution. Everyone is a decision maker. There is no back room.

The process is definitive because the visual organization of ideas posted on a wall reveals the emergent themes in an unambiguous way. The themes are not defined by some elegant master stroke. They are defined a multitude of small binary decisions—is this like this, or not? When each individual decision is sound, the aggregate of all those decisions is also sound. The participants watch this process unfold and seem to intuitively appreciate its visual logic.

The multi-voting process is another rapid, visual, and transparent process that posts data from every participant and makes the collective preferences visible to all. Participants are given an equal number of adhesive dots and a chance to privately reflect, in their seats, on their preferences. Group members then walk up together and post their dots in targets next to the themes that most capture their interest. Instantly, there is a clear visual record of a complex set of individual judgments that collectively express the preferences of the group as a whole.

Community Members Post Ideas and Choose the Best

Let's return to our community conversation about kids and learning. The aspirations of individuals have been written out on adhesive notes.

Now, at their tables, the participants are sharing these ideas with each other. They are posting them on a flip chart pad or a nearby wall. They are actively looking for the common ideas among them and physically clustering those sticky notes into groups of similar ideas.

This is highly engaging because it is simultaneously a physical, intellectual, visual act.

- **Physical.** People are getting up and walking around. People are writing and sorting.
- **Intellectual.** People are thinking and talking. People are organizing concepts. People are analyzing pros and cons. People are choosing.
- **Visual.** People are writing, drawing, arranging their dots, and looking. Participants enjoy making visual order of the chaos of individual elements. They cap off their categories with labels that express the shared elements of the ideas beneath.

In less than half an hour, they have heard everyone's aspirations, posted them, discovered the shared themes, and expressed these new insights visually, through spatial order and hierarchy.

At this point I invited representatives from the tables to bring forward their best two or three ideas on posters about half the size of a standard flip chart page. Before the meeting, we covered an entire wall of the school cafeteria with brown paper. Now table representatives were coming forward in waves, posting their ideas on the Vision Wall.

We grouped these ideas again, using the same process as had been used at the tables, just on a grander scale. The earliest ideas mostly claimed their own territory. The later ideas tended to find a home near a similar idea expressed earlier. No one was in charge of setting the themes—they just emerged. Sometimes the reporters from individual tables offered ideas that had already been mentioned apologetically, as if a new and unique idea would be better. I encouraged them heartily, reassuring them that redundancy, in this case, was our friend. The emergence of similar ideas from many tables, all designed by their seating assignments to ensure diversity, was a really, really good sign. And everyone in the room could see it.

Nine themes emerged that morning from the aspirations of the 130 participants. The magic of these simple themes is that they represent common ground among a large, public gathering of people with very different values and political perspectives:

- To provide a rich variety of curriculum choices.
- To create an environment that encourages high expectations for students and teachers.
- To provide adequate tools and resources.
- To think critically, to problem solve, to plan, and to become lifelong learners.
- To promote a strong sense of students' own competence and value.
- To create a reciprocal, supportive environment between school and community.
- To develop a reputation for being best in class.
- To make a positive contribution to society.
- To create a safe and respectful environment with trained adult role models.

"You can want it all, but you have to make choices," we said next. Finding a large base of common ground is wonderful, but having it be too large can be overwhelming. So we ask individuals to choose. Each participant received three adhesive dots to use in expressing their top preferences. The participants quickly found their way to the front of the room, placed their dots, and returned to their seats. Multi-voting, like the earlier sorting task, is simultaneously a physical, intellectual, and visual act. It took only minutes, and yet the results were dramatic and transparent. The participants gave 80 percent of their votes to the first five themes listed above. A widely polarized community had found deep, focused common ground in mere hours.

ENERGIZING: INVOLVE EVERYONE TO ENSURE FOLLOW-THROUGH

Grounded Visioning is fun. People enjoy it. They walk away energized. It is fun because it is fast. It moves so quickly you would think people might get dizzy. It doesn't wear out its welcome. It is fun because it starts with stories. And everyone loves stories. It is fun because it is positive. And people feel good when they focus on the positive. It is fun because it is visual and physical. People love being

---

Simple yet Smart

Don't underestimate Grounded Visioning because of its simplicity. Its simplicity makes it powerful. Because people can easily understand and use Grounded Visioning, they are more likely to buy into the process. Everyone saves time because Grounded Visioning is straightforward. And participants think about the vision, rather than getting tangled in details of the method.

Remember Oliver Wendell Holmes, who said, "I would not give a fig for the simplicity on this side of complexity, but I would give my life for the simplicity on the other side of complexity." Grounded Visioning is simplicity from the other side of complexity.

---

involved. They love seeing things emerge; it is like a puzzle being solved. They love getting up and moving when it is time to vote.

It is energizing because everyone's input is important. Everyone's input is heard, and everyone's input matters. It is energizing because it honors the past, and people feel appreciated. It is energizing because it allows people to imagine the future they want, and then enables them to see that others very likely share their hopes and dreams. It is energizing because most people want only the best for themselves and their organization, and this gives them the chance to express it. It is energizing because it lets people know that their good work will be valued and built upon in action plans and next steps.

50 Percent Volunteer to Make the Vision Real

Back at our town, the community conversation was coming to a close. With more time, participants could have gathered in small groups to organize for implementation planning around aspects of the vision that most attracted their interest. A Grounded Visioning session always closes with action plans for next steps because people need to know how their good work will be put to use. We don't always have time to make action plans in the moment, but we can at least spell out when they will be made, and by whom.

In this town, that meant forming work groups focused on the top three priorities—curriculum, student competence, and community relations—to detail action plans over the summer. On the spot, a startling 65 people volunteered to help flesh out the learning goals. As part of their role in planning the conversation, the superintendent and members of the school committee had mapped out two tools to help potential volunteers understand the scope of their commitment. The first was a generic charge for the work groups that everyone hoped would form out of the conversation. The second was a proposed calendar of presumed next steps leading to school committee approval in the fall.

Key process elements of the goal teams' charge included:

- Overall purpose (create action plan).
- Results expected (objectives, measures, action plans, etc.).
- Key task completion dates.
- Resources provided (from sponsors, including leadership training).
- Constraints (givens and parameters).
- Sponsorship (leadership role of superintendent and school committee).
- Key approval points.

Note that neither the superintendent nor the school committee knew the content of the goals in advance. They just knew that some goals would emerge and that some people would want to work on them. Their charge laid out a generic set of steps to bring those goals from ideas to final recommendations.

Their work done, the participants flocked to a potluck lunch. An eighth grader told how he had originally come just to play tenor saxophone with the school band at the start of the meeting but had gotten caught up in the discussions and stayed the whole morning. A parent chimed in, "This was the most amazing organization of so many thoughts." The superintendent could be heard saying, "We're planting the seeds. We're finding the themes and the voices that want to be heard. Finding consensus among community members is vital to providing the school system the town wants. It's a daring act for a community to come together and dream together."

NOTES

1. Marvin R. Weisbord and Sandra Janoff, *Future Search: An Action Guide to Finding Common Ground in Organizations & Communities* (San Francisco: Berrett-Koehler, 1995); also see www.futuresearch.net (accessed May 27, 2008).

2. Bernard J. Mohr and Jane Magruder Watkins, *Essentials of Appreciative Inquiry: A Roadmap for Creating Positive Futures* (Waltham, MA: Pegasus Communications, Inc., 2002).

3. P.M. Senge, *The Fifth Discipline. The Art and Practice of the Learning Organization* (London: Random House, 1990), 9.

PART II

How to Create Your
Grounded Vision

—————— 4 ——————

Get Set for a Grounded Visioning Session

Planning happens at the Grounded Visioning session—not before.

The past is a source of knowledge, and the future is a source of hope. Love of the past implies faith in the future.

—Stephen Ambrose[1]

The beauty of a Grounded Visioning session is that planning one for an individual team takes very little preparation. You need to do everything you would to arrange any kind of meeting: reserve the space, make sure seating is adequate, order coffee and snacks. But you don't need to do a lot of pre-session planning.

In fact, it's important that you not do so. Grounded Visioning is by its nature diagnostic, which means that it reveals what the team needs as it proceeds, and inclusive, which means that you should not try to determine or guide the outcome too strongly.

To get ready, you need to decide first whether Grounded Visioning can help your team.

Then you need to decide whether to use the "small group" or "large group" version of the method.

Assuming you are working with a small group, you are then ready to follow these five simple steps:

- Set the context.
- Invite your team.
- Identify a leader.
- Foster a safe environment.
- Prepare the space.

DECIDE IF NOW IS THE TIME FOR GROUNDED VISIONING

Consider the typical team or work group. Perhaps your team is coming off a high from a mission recently accomplished, and you sense that it needs a new challenge. Maybe your team is functioning just fine in terms of its performance, but you sense that it can go deeper in looking at how it works together and how its members can gain greater satisfaction from their work. These high-performing teams may be ready for a visioning tune-up.

Teams that are struggling are also candidates for a Grounded Visioning session. I often consult with clients concerned about teams where there is infighting, competition over turf, and distrust. Invariably, these teams have lost sight of their purpose and vision. They have forgotten who their customer is and why they exist. Deprived of the focus that a clear purpose and vision provide, they fall to fighting among themselves. These struggling teams need to refocus, quickly, on the common goals that unite them, the goals that are greater than any of their individual needs and wants.

Maybe your team is not yet fighting with itself. Maybe it is just drifting a bit. You may hear the dreaded phrases, "We lack vision" and "We don't know where we are going." Sometimes a team simply forgets how good it can be. It gets rusty or complacent. It indulges in worry and negativity that are really beneath it. It needs a chance to remember its strengths, not just its shortcomings, and to celebrate what it does well. It needs a chance to shake off its sluggishness and wake up to the challenges before it.

Special Considerations for Organizations and Communities

Moving beyond work groups to organizations and communities, the reasons to engage in a Grounded Visioning session are similar, yet invariably more complex. I have worked with organizations at the top of their game that seek the vision to keep their best people forever challenged and their supporters forever inspired. It is an honor and a privilege to work with leaders who appreciate the vitality that breathes into organizations through vision—even when nothing is overtly "wrong."

In contrast, I have worked with organizations on the ropes, trying to bounce back from disasters and the wreckage of broken dreams. Perhaps they have new leadership and a new generation of workers. The only way to turn their fortunes around is to ask their supporters to take a risk and dream together. Without first imaging their success, they will never attain it.

In the public arena, I have worked with cities and towns that have a proud record of achievement and are merely coming together once again to find their next target for success. And I have worked with communities in distress, divided, fighting against hopelessness to find common ground.

Leaders Who Choose the Future

From work group to small volunteer team to large organization to geographic community, one common characteristic holds true. In almost every case there is a leader (or group of leaders) who wants the future to be different from the past. In almost every case there is a leader (or group of leaders) who believes in collaboration. As Ben Franklin put it, "We must all hang together, or most assuredly we will all hang separately." In almost every case there is a leader (or group of leaders) willing to take a risk.

I like to think of these leaders as fundamentally different from other leaders. They have made a surprising choice. Let's call it where they choose to stand. Some leaders stand in the present, which is a product of the past, and thus hold their team to expectations that are consistent with past experience. This generally means asking team members to do more of the same. This stance is not visionary, but it is comfortable, and many teams claim to like it, up to a point.

Other leaders choose to stand in the future, a world of infinite possibility, and expect their teams to join them there. This means asking the team to stretch, grow, and create. It means holding them to a higher standard. They are not victims of their past, and their future is not preordained. It is up to the team to create the future together, based on how they are when they are at their best. This stance is visionary, but it is not always comfortable.

I believe that every team has the capacity, and ultimately the desire, to embrace the future in this way. Unfortunately, not every team is lucky enough to have a leader willing to take it there. Teams with leaders willing to sponsor an open-ended look at what might be are lucky.

CHOOSE EITHER THE "SMALL GROUP" OR THE "LARGE GROUP" METHOD

Before the session, you must decide whether to follow the "small group" or "large group" version of the method (see chapters 6 and 7, and 8 and 9, respectively). That is, do you want everyone in the room to work together all during the Grounded Visioning session? That means using the small group method. Or is your group so large that you will need to divide into table groups that work in parallel? That means using the large group version.

A small team of 8 to 12 is obviously a small group. Everyone can fit around a single table. So you go with the small group process design. Read more about that in chapters 6 and 7.

A big gathering of 120 or more is obviously a large group. Participants sit at round tables of 8. They function as a series of small groups working in parallel. So you go with the large group process design. Read more about that in chapters 8 and 9.

But what if your team of 12 members wants to invite 12 allies to join in? You cannot fit around one table. Logic suggests that you go with the large group method, using three groups of 8. If you have any doubts about your facilitation expertise, you should choose the large group design. When you break down into table groups, you distribute more of the burden of running the session throughout the group.

If you feel confident about managing such a big group, you may consider working with this larger group using the small group format. People still start the session working in pairs. They still toss out their attractions and share stories with everyone. The whole group still articulates some statements about how they are when they are at their very best. And everyone individually shares and posts their aspirations. You just have more of everything to process. If you can pull it off, it can be very exciting and energizing.

But if the thought of managing all those inputs for a group of two dozen makes you dizzy, go the simpler route, choose the large group method, and let the table work groups do a lot of the organizing for you.

SET THE CONTEXT

Let's assume you are planning a session for your team of a dozen or less, and will use the small group method. You don't need the typical "meeting to plan the meeting" at which participants define desired outcomes for the session. Those outcomes are givens—the Grounded Visioning method yields a Grounded Vision. It yields team cohesion, shared vision, and clarity on next steps.

It isn't necessary to train anyone, or coach them, to enable their full participation. It is possible to just choose to hold one, schedule it, have people show up, and find that it works just fine.

Interviewing Everyone Not Necessary

There is no need for a consultant or manager to diagnose problems in secret in advance of the meeting. Team members won't need to sit and politely listen to an expert listing of their "issues" that "need to be worked," like schoolchildren at report-card time.

When a consultant does interviews before a planning session, the consultant is the only person who sees the team as a whole. Interviewing gives the consultant tremendous knowledge, power, and authority. This power has a price, however, in that it disempowers the team. When analysis and decisions are handed down in this way, you send a powerful negative message to the team: that it is not capable of identifying its own solutions or mapping its own set of challenges.

Ideally, a healthy team process involves the whole team in real time, thus building relationships among team members and giving greater information—and therefore power—to its members. A healthy team process builds core team strengths and empowers the team to define its own challenges and set its own aspirations.

This is why Grounded Visioning gathers all the information it needs to be successful within the confines of the meeting itself, in real time, in a way that is public, yet safe. The process affirms the team's ability to define its own challenges and set its own aspirations. Team members make their own choices and feel committed to the success of the vision.

If you have time, however, there are two ways you can improve the experience and make the most of your meeting time. You set the context for the meeting by providing background information and by deciding if there are any topics outside the scope of the visioning session.

What Are Your Guiding Ideas?

Your guiding ideas are any existing statements of mission, values, philosophy, etc. that define your reason for being and frame the boundaries of who you are, and what makes you different from others. These documents can be shared with the team in advance of the session as a refresher and guide.

These documents frame the context in which the vision will be set. Mission in my view, for example, defines why you exist and whom you serve. It states your reason for being, or ultimate aim, and the beneficiary of your efforts (what Peter Drucker calls "the primary customer"[2]). As such it is something that defines your purpose and should not change easily.

Many teams or organizations also have explicit statements defining what they value. Some of the wonderful ones we've encountered over the years are "Better together," "The plan is the boss," and "Nothing is impossible!" These words are outer reminders of inner states of being that help people choose one action—the right one for the company, organization, or community—over another.

Are Some Issues Outside Your Scope?

Decide if there are any nonnegotiable limits to the vision. These can be either elements it must include or areas into which it cannot enter. Sharing givens in a frank, honest way, perhaps with some explanation as to why they are givens and not negotiable, is almost always received with respect. People accept that work comes with limits, just like a game comes with rules. They just want to know how the game is played. They don't want to be reprimanded after the fact for proposing something that was always out of bounds anyway, only no one bothered to tell them.

For example, a design team may specify the given that new ventures must build on the team's existing core competencies. A nonprofit may specify that new programs must come with an associated source of funding or subsidy. A community may specify that new development being envisioned must comply with smart growth principles.

INVITE YOUR TEAM

For a small work group, it's easy to choose participants in the Grounded Visioning. You just include everyone on your team.

In addition, you might want to invite friends and allies. By working with your team only, you build its sense of identity and cohesion. By working with the team's collaborators—and even its customers—you get the chance to build an expanded sense of what success really looks like and get others to buy into the team's success.

When your team members are willing to show up and play together, you already have the most important ingredient of a successful Grounded Visioning session.

IDENTIFY A LEADER

You can facilitate a Grounded Visioning session for your team. This book is based on that premise. You'll want to give yourself permission to wear two hats: one as meeting leader, the other as meeting participant. The team needs your contribution too! If that is too much to juggle, try using one of these strategies:

- Ask different members of the team to prepare to lead different parts of the session.
- Ask a leader of another team to lead your session and offer to return the favor.
- Ask an internal development consultant to lead your session, if your organization is lucky enough to have one.
- Ask an external development consultant to lead your session, if you can afford it.

Use the instructions in this book and the templates in Appendices to organize the meeting.

FOSTER A SAFE ENVIRONMENT

We all know that some work environments are safer than others and that people's willingness to risk rests in large measure on their feelings of being safe. How can we consistently create a safe space for sharing about the future in a team?

Creating a Grounded Vision is a structured process that builds respect for personal safety into every one of its steps. You build this environment of safety step-by-step just by following the design:

- Set ground rules for working together collaboratively at the beginning of the visioning session. These rules guide people toward acting in ways which build and sustain a sense of safety. For example, the simple statement "speak up, yet speak briefly" reminds us that we are in the team for a good reason and if we don't "speak up," an important contribution to the group will be lost. Conversely, if we don't "speak briefly," we will be taking air time from our team mates.
- Individuals work immediately in pairs, which is a more private and intimate forum for exchange than speaking with the whole group.
- Interviews in pairs begin by describing their attractions to the team or the work at hand, which rapidly creates a context of shared motivation and connection.
- Individuals in their paired interviews focus on what works, rather than on what doesn't, which typically feels less risky to share.
- Individuals share their attractions in a brainstorming forum, where it is not clear whether they are sharing their own ideas or those of their partner.

Ground Rules Help Everyone Participate to Their Full Potential

- One person speaks at a time.
- Listen to understand, not judge.
- Speak up, yet speak briefly.
- Balance advocacy with inquiry.
- Have fun while getting lots done!

- Individuals only share their dreams, hopes, and aspirations publicly with the whole group after they have first shared them privately. There is no judgment or evaluation of those contributions at the time they are shared.
- Individual contributions of aspirations, once written, are added without identifying names to a newly emerging Vision Wall and merged anonymously with the work of others.
- The expression of preferences for one set of ideas over another is done by votes with unmarked dots, all at once, to heighten a sense of anonymity and show that in the building of the future vision, everyone has an equal voice.

These design characteristics help teams with trust issues that might falter or freeze in conversations about the future to speak frankly, without reprisal, in a Grounded Visioning session. Each of the small choices listed here—and built into the design of a Grounded Visioning session—contribute, in a subtle way, to this sense of safety.

PREPARE THE SPACE

The preparations you do in the meeting space are driven by the experience you are hoping to create with your participants. You will want to foster eye contact and exchange, so chairs set in a semicircle or in a U-shape around a table work better than chairs set in classroom-style rows. You will want to create a shared visual focus for the group as it works, so orienting the semicircle or U toward a large, blank wall works best. Natural light coming in from the sides or the rear is a wonderful plus.

You will want to set the context at the start of the meeting by sharing an agenda, ground rules, and possibly some of the team's guiding ideas in some form. Often this information is written out on flip chart posters that are placed in advance on the wall that is central to everyone's focus.

You will want to have lots of flip chart paper on hand to record the attractions and high points that will be shared. Many meeting facilities offer flip chart paper on freestanding easels. I prefer working without easels, using the paper taped one sheet at a time, in multiple layers, directly on the wall. This creates a large supply of paper, taped and ready to go, at the front of the room. In addition, it removes the easels from our space at the front of the room, which gives us more room to work.

In addition, you will want to have large sheets of brown kraft or butcher paper ready to go on the wall to create a home for everyone's aspirations, written on sticky notes. We like to create a surface that is 4 feet tall and 12 feet wide for a work group of a dozen.

Post this paper in the reverse order in which you will need it. First put up the butcher paper because you will be using that last. Next, cover the butcher paper with the flip chart sheets because you will be using them in the middle. Last, you put up your agenda and context-setting posters because you will be using them first.

You will want to have pads and pens or pencils ready for the interviewing exercise. You will want markers and adhesive notes ready for the dreams, hopes, and aspirations exercise. You will want adhesive dots and scissors ready for the multi-voting exercise.

Now, you are ready to roll.

NOTES

1. Harriet Rubin, "Past Track to the Future," *Fast Company* (May 2001): 166.
2. Peter F. Drucker, *The Five Most Important Questions You Will Ever Ask about Your Non-profit Organization: The Drucker Foundation Self-Assessment Tool for Nonprofit Organizations* (San Francisco: Jossey-Bass Publishers, 1993).

5

Get Set: Large Groups Need a Planning Committee

Even very large groups can work collaboratively and transparently.

[T]he more power you give a single individual in the face of complexity and uncertainty, the more likely it is that bad decisions will get made.

—James Surowiecki[1]

You will be using the large group version of the Grounded Visioning method most every time you want to convene more than two dozen people. With more people involved there will be far more moving parts to coordinate. The more complex logistics alone dictate that you need to do more advance work. A planning committee ensures that you use your large group meeting time most effectively.

The planning committee should mirror the diversity you want in the room, more or less. That ensures that the diverse viewpoints that are likely to come up in the actual session are likely to come up in planning it, too. That gives you a chance to build consensus and foster collaboration before you ever start the meeting. Plus you'll encounter fewer surprises and have a more smoothly organized meeting. A diverse planning committee also helps build credibility for the event. Participants look at the list of organizers and recognize someone who shares their view of the world, which makes them think, "If she is helping organize this, then it can't be too bad!"

The planning committee may need to meet several times to get ready. Or the committee may need to meet only once before and once after. The planning committee has four main tasks:

- Affirm the session's desired outcomes, agenda, and leadership.
- Identify and invite the right participants.

- Plan and manage site logistics.
- Plan communications and follow-through.

AFFIRM DESIRED OUTCOMES AND AGENDA

The planning committee's first task—defining the session's desired outcomes and agenda—is relatively simple. Frequently, the meeting's leaders or facilitators assume responsibility for this task.

A Grounded Visioning session exists only for one reason (shared vision!) and comes with a set agenda. Planning committees can follow the set four-hour agenda in Appendix 4 and probably will find that it requires little alteration.

Reading the cases throughout this book will give you a sense of the elasticity of the method, and how it can be successfully adapted for a variety of unique situations.

Principles for Large Group Agendas

I let my work with large groups be informed by a set of beliefs that guided the masterful work of Kathy Dannemiller.[2]

- Our process and plans must always be client focused and client driven. The client must "own" the process and the outcomes. Change can happen fast throughout the "whole system" when the whole system participates in change. We strive to involve as many interested parties as is practical.
- All activities need to add to the common database of participant knowledge about their challenge and situation. Adults are motivated to solve real problems and address real challenges.
- All activities need to build the team. Never do something for the individual that hurts the group and never do something for the group that hurts the individual.
- People self-manage their work and use dialogue, not problem-solving, as the main means of communicating. That means helping each other do the tasks and taking responsibility for our perceptions and actions.
- Achieving real change means seeing the world in a new way. People must see things differently if they are going to do things differently.
- Good process is based on sound theory of how adults and organizations change. We manage the energy in the room and empower the participants to take action.
- Effective meeting process can and will lead to action. The right choices for next steps emerge out of an effective process.

These beliefs are embedded in the design choices that comprise the steps of the large group version of Grounded Visioning. They shape the experience of participants in both subtle and significant ways, leading to outcomes that participants find refreshing, enlivening, and uplifting.

Identify the Leader or Facilitator

It is possible to lead a large group meeting by yourself, even if you do not have extensive facilitation experience, for two reasons:

- The meeting design and materials in this book give you a firm structure to follow.
- The large group process uses many small groups working in parallel with volunteer facilitators. They do much of the heavy lifting.

That said, the prospect of being in charge of a big group can be a bit intimidating. You can always bring in an internal resource, an external resource, or a skilled volunteer. This individual (or individuals) can help the planning committee adjust the proposed set agenda to meet any unique aspects of your group's situation.

INVITE THE RIGHT PARTICIPANTS

Frequently the whole planning committee identifies and invites participants for a large group meeting. Or you might have a subcommittee of the planning committee handle this.

Large group planners often enjoy the challenge of filling the room with the right people. I like to draw a big circle on some flip chart paper, representing a round table, surrounded by eight or so chairs. Then I ask: "Who needs to be at the table?" You're looking for stakeholders, defined simply as people with a stake in the future of the organization or community. Look for people who encompass the three Is: people who are *informed* about the organization or community, people who will feel the *impact* of what is being discussed, and people who can *influence* our ability to achieve our dreams.

We make a list of stakeholder groups, using adhesive notes so we can later change our minds or group them together in higher order clusters. Our goal is to map the whole system. After generating a thorough list of participant categories, we return to the number of chairs at the table. Here our goal is to create a "max-mix" at every table, that is, the maximum diversity possible—a microcosm of the macrocosm that is the organization or community. This ensures that every proposal that emerges from a work group table is vetted

Figure 5.1

Invite representatives of all points of view: Aim to create the maximum diversity at every table.

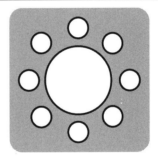

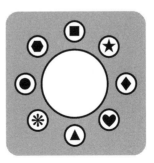

Illustration by Cindy Murphy.

through a diverse set of lenses. If it passes muster with that diverse group, it will probably appeal to the broad cross section represented by the room (or whole system).

Keeping track of the chairs at the table helps us be realistic about how many people can attend. With room for eight seats at every table and 10 tables in the room, we have room for 80 participants. Put another way, we have space for a maximum of eight stakeholder groups composed of 10 representatives each. If we find that one group is much larger and more dominant in the life of the organization than another, we can give them two chairs at the table. That gives us seven stakeholder groups, six with 10 representatives and one with 20, and so on.

Sometimes planners decide to add or subtract chairs; sometimes, they add or subtract tables. Remember that the more tables you add, the more time you need to allow everyone to give reports. In the Grounded Visioning format, there are only two rounds of quick reports from tables, so I tend to err on the side of inclusion.

Sometimes, even for larger groups, participants choose themselves, as you saw in the example of the public school district in Chapter 3 and will see again with the Downtown Center Associates in Chapter 7. In these situations, you find out how many participants there are only at the actual start of the Grounded Visioning session.

Define Invitation Strategies

Once the planners have identified the stakeholder groups that need to be present and in what numbers, you can define invitation strategies. These may be different for different constituencies. A typical college, for example, has stakeholder groups like faculty, staff, trustees, students, alumni, business leaders, community leaders, political leaders, and educational leaders. Students may be asked to volunteer themselves as potential participants, with the president making final selections based on applications. Faculty may meet in departments to vote representative selections for their allotted slots. The president may personally invite business leaders and distinguished alumni.

The planning group needs, at a minimum, to identify individuals responsible for identifying, inviting, and confirming participants in each of the key stakeholder groups. Two or three people need to compile these lists and assemble table assignments that give us the "max-mix" of all stakeholder groups.

PLAN AND MANAGE SITE LOGISTICS

A third major responsibility for the planning committee is planning and managing site logistics. You might want a logistics subcommittee to decide key logistical questions, such as the location, date, and timing of the event (see checklist in this chapter). They must find a site that works suitably for the meeting's purposes and arrange for all equipment, supplies, and refreshments at the site.

These site conditions help ensure success:

- Adequate space to greet and register the participants as they arrive, perhaps in a hall or anteroom outside the meeting space.
- Adequate room for participants to sit comfortably at round tables in groups of eight, with space between tables and tables and between tables and walls.
- Adequate room for the creation of a Vision Wall on which the group's work will be posted, sorted, and prioritized.
- Adequate room for the meeting leaders to work in the front of the room and for the function staff to set out any refreshments.
- Natural light coming from the side or rear or above.
- Sound systems for amplifying voices with microphones.

Registration

At large meetings, lots of individuals are trying to find their way into the same space at the same time to do some work together. Meeting organizers need space in which to greet them, to hand out name tags, to distribute the participant workbook (either at registration or at the table), and to hand out table assignments or seating instructions.

Participant Workbooks

Large group versions of the Grounded Visioning method work partly because the process is made transparent by materials that are shared in writing with every participant. Sometimes these workbooks are distributed at the registration table. Sometimes they are waiting at the table. Typically they contain the following:

- Background materials that set the context (like "guiding ideas").
- Handouts with an agenda, ground rules, work group leadership roles, and a description of how this meeting differs from typical meetings.
- Worksheets for each small group task at the tables.
- Lists of participants and contact information.

See Appendices for sample handouts and worksheets.

Round Tables

I strongly recommend round tables because they provide excellent sight lines to everyone in the work group. They also convey a sense of interpersonal equality that is in keeping with the spirit of Grounded Visioning. I have led meetings in rooms with all sorts of tables—and even without any tables at all—but round tables are best. I strongly suggest tables of eight. It is a large enough group to be diverse, yet small enough to be efficient.

Some meeting sponsors have pushed me to seat people at tables of 10, rather than add more tables. They are aware of the time it takes for more tables to report and to participate in the visioning process. Still, if meeting sponsors want lots of

Who Does What: Planning Team Tasks and Roles

One way that planning teams assign roles

Planning Team

- Identifies key questions, outcomes, tasks for the session.
- Identifies participants and selection criteria.
- Invites individuals as needed.
- Approves session date, time, location.
- Selects strategy for public relations, session proceedings.
- Approves all correspondence and public relations.
- Manages pre-/post-session activities and the event itself.
- Provides input and strategy for assuring follow-through of session output.

Participants Subcommittee

- Presents participant and alternate slate to planning team.
- Sends invitation and confirmation letters.
- Tracks participant commitments and invites alternates.
- Assures full participation in the session.
- Provides list of session participants and affiliation for workbook.
- Develops list of table assignments for mixed group tables.

Logistics Subcommittee

- Assures site meets room specifications.
- Plans menu and refreshments.
- Devises wall space if needed.
- Provides all equipment and supplies for session.
- Assures that participant workbooks are printed and ready for session.
- Provides administrative assistance at registration.
- Provides name badges for participants for all sessions.
- Coordinates meeting room set up.

Public Relations Subcommittee

- Drafts invitation and confirmation letters.
- Develops and carries out pre/post media and internal communications campaign.
- Assigns recorders/videographers, if needed.
- Provides necessary equipment for recording event, if needed.
- Follows through on timely proceedings.

people and they want to accomplish a lot of work in a short amount of time, something has to give. There is a trade-off: Adding more people to each table makes it possible to invite more participants without adding the additional reporting time of more tables. But a larger group at each table makes it harder for people at the individual tables to do their business, particularly when they are surrounded by nearby overcrowded tables.

Sometimes meeting sponsors can predict that 2 out of every 10 people who say they will come to a meeting won't show up. For this reason, we sometimes go with tables of 10, but this is not my preference.

Infrequently, meeting sponsors want to seat fewer people at each table. Tables of six can also work, if the tables at the site are small and the size of the whole group doesn't make the reports from this larger number of tables too cumbersome.

Vision Wall

Although the large group is divided so everyone can contribute efficiently, you still need a way for everyone to come together in a collaborative way for the sorting and voting. It's crucial that large groups have a shared visual focus, what I call the Vision Wall. This is just a large flat wall that you can cover with brown butcher paper to record high points, dreams, and aspirations.

Make sure there is some floor space in front of this wall, so the facilitators can record comments and representatives from each table can report in the front of the room. If you have a wonderful space but the wall is covered with art, sconces, etc., you can purchase 4' × 8' sheets of 3/16" foam core. Taped together, these sheets create light, rigid walls that will transform a cluttered wall into a usable work surface.

Space for Meeting Leaders

The meeting leader or leaders typically need a small table for their materials and supplies at the front of the room. They typically also need one or two flip chart easels, pads, and markers for displaying key posters, or making key notes.

Natural Light

Natural light relaxes and invigorates participants in an effortless, unseen way. Unfortunately, you may have to make do without it. If so, consider adding brief enlivening activities, or stretch breaks, to bring up the energy in the room as needed.

Sound Systems

Most large group meetings require some kind of sound amplification. I strongly recommend handheld, wireless microphones. They make it easy to share the power of the microphone with participants. And they equalize the contributions of people with softer voices.

PLAN COMMUNICATIONS AND FOLLOW-THROUGH

The planning committee's fourth task is to think about public relations, both before and after the meeting, and follow-through. It needs to prepare and distribute any briefing materials in advance and to prepare participant materials complete with handouts, worksheets, and participant list.

There is an opportunity to present, or re-present, the team, organization, or community, to its stakeholders. What are the key messages, and materials, that should be shared with these stakeholders?

Then, after the Grounded Visioning session, there is an opportunity to share the successes of the event afterward in a way that builds the brand and reputation of the group. How will we share these successes with those who came? How will we share that story with those who wanted to come but couldn't? And with those who should have wanted to come but didn't? How will we want to document the event in a way that makes it easy to share it with others?

How will we follow up the results of the session, translate its visions into actions, and integrate those plans with tactics and operations? (These questions are addressed in more detail in Chapter 10, "Vision into Action.")

NOTES

1. James Surowiecki, *The Wisdom of Crowds—Why the Many Are Smarter than the Few and How Collective Wisdom Shapes Business, Economies, Societies, and Nations* (New York: Doubleday, 2004), 220.

2. Dannemiller Tyson Associates, *Real-Time Strategic Change: A Consultant Guide to Large-Scale Meetings* (Ann Arbor, MI: Dannemiller Tyson Associates, 1994), 20.

6

Step-by-Step: Grounded Visioning for Small Groups

Specific instructions and stated time limits help groups quickly create a vision.

The only limit to our realization of tomorrow will be our doubts of today.
—Franklin Delano Roosevelt

I f your team or work group has between 6 and 24 members, you can use the simplest Grounded Visioning template, what I call the "small group version." With 24 or fewer people, productive dialogue can take place among the group as a whole.

Table 6.1 shows the basic agenda for a two-hour Grounded Visioning session for a small group.

WELCOME, ORIENT, AND EXPLAIN TASK

The leader of the work group or the sponsor of the meeting typically welcomes participants, explains the purpose of the gathering in an upbeat way, and makes any necessary introductions. This should take about 10 minutes.

If there is a facilitator for the session, the person in this role typically affirms the desired outcomes and agenda for the session, explains the facilitator's role, and articulates any ground rules governing how everyone will work together.

We use "OARRs" as a memory aid to help us plan this part of the meeting, an acronym popularized by the Grove Consultants International.[1] It stands for *outcomes, agenda, roles, and rules.* Clarifying these four things helps everyone work in alignment throughout the session, like oarsmen rowing well together.

Outcomes. In discussing outcomes, we typically distinguish between an overall purpose—a broad goal toward which progress is made in the time

Table 6.1
Small Group Agenda
Make the Six Steps Happen

Time (minutes)	Task
10	*Assemble your stakeholders:* Welcome, orient, and explain task
15	*Ignite your spark:* Conduct appreciative interviews in pairs
	• Attractions
	• High points
	• Dreams, hopes, and aspirations
	• Reasons for optimism
15	*Share best practices*/attractions: Share attractions briefly in large group
30	*Share best practices*/high points: Share high point stories briefly in large group
	Summarize themes
30	*Share your dreams:* Post dreams, hopes, and aspirations
	• Individuals write on adhesive notes
	• Individuals read, link to like ideas, and post
15	*Select the best:*
	• Multi-vote
	• Reflect
5	*Plan next steps:*
	• Share reasons for optimism

allotted—and desired outcomes—tangible objectives that are fully realized. For example, our overall purpose is to create a shared vision and sense of direction for the team. Our more narrow desired outcomes might be to share what's best about the team in a fun and positive way, to define elements of a shared vision, and to create an action plan for next steps.

Agenda. The facilitator should briefly introduce the agenda, indicating which activities serve to deliver which outcomes and how the group's time will be allocated.

Roles. In defining the facilitator role, we often refer to the root meaning of the word "facilitate," which is "to make easy." It is the facilitator's job to make it easy for the team to accomplish its outcomes. We remind them that we serve at their pleasure, and that this is their time, not ours.

Rules. We introduce ground rules to help every participant get the most value from the session. Ground rules make it safe for team members to participate fully. They remind participants how to conduct themselves to get the most out of a meeting. Some of our favorites are:

- One person speaks at a time.
- Speak up, yet speak briefly.
- Balance advocacy with inquiry.
- Have fun while getting lots done.

Sometimes, we just use an elegantly simple rule favored by one of our clients: "Builds, not bombs."

CONDUCT APPRECIATIVE INTERVIEWS IN PAIRS

The first task of a Grounded Visioning session is a short interview done in pairs inspired directly by the methodology known as Appreciative Inquiry (for more information on this method, see Chapter 12, "The Power of the Positive"). You can accomplish this in about 15 minutes.

Usually people speak to the person sitting next to them, but sometimes special pairs form. If half a team is new, and the other half is more senior, for example, you might want to ask people to pair up as newbies and veterans. If half the group is from a newly acquired company, and the other half is from the parent company, you might pair up as one of each. The idea is to foster an exchange of diverse views and to build bridges across differences. If everyone in the room knows everyone else very well, remind them that they will be asking some questions that they don't typically ask. Tell them not to be surprised if they hear and learn something new from someone they assumed they knew very well.

The interview is simple to explain and easy to do. In introducing the interview process, you should outline it in terms that are easily understood by the participants. For example:

> For starters, we would like you to partner with the person sitting next to you and interview each other in turn. We want you to listen carefully and take notes, so you'll need a pad of paper and a pen or pencil. There are many ways of learning about a person and a team, and a typical way is to ask what hurts, like a doctor might, and to explore those problems in detail. While that can be a very useful way to look at things, we also find it brings our energy down, and we need that energy to address the very real challenges we face. So in this interview, we'll go a different direction, and ask just about what works. We'll be unabashedly positive in our approach. Think of it as a short research study on best practices in this team. We find that it builds our energy and enables us to take on even bigger challenges successfully.

Four Important Questions

Next, invite participants to ask four questions that draw information out of their partners:

- **Attractions.** What attracted you to this team, and keeps you?
- **High points.** In your experience of this team, think of a time when you felt most committed, most proud to be part of it, most engaged, most alive and connected. Tell that story and what made it so great.
- **Dreams, hopes, and aspirations.** Imagine a positive future for this team. What are three dreams, hopes, or aspirations that you have for what this team might do or be?
- **Reasons for optimism.** What is one reason for optimism that those dreams, hopes, and aspirations might actually come to pass?

To keep the session on track, it's good to remind participants of time constraints, for example:

"You have 15 minutes. I'll ring this bell at the halfway point and again at the end. Any questions about what we want you to do? No? Then please begin."

With these simple instructions, the pairs are off and running, and the music of animated human conversation soon fills the room.

The interview serves several important functions. Delightfully, it functions as an icebreaker, even in groups where people know each other well, allowing us to build community while getting work done. It gathers data about the team and its process in a deliberately appreciative way, building a context of positive thoughts and success. Most important, it serves as the spark plug for our visioning process, supplying the energy that feeds the success of the entire enterprise.

As the facilitator, you can join in if there happens to be an odd number of persons in the room or finish your preparations for the discussion that follows immediately after. You'll want markers and several sheets of flip chart paper ready to go.

SHARE ATTRACTIONS WITH THE WHOLE GROUP

By sharing attractions—what brought members to this team and keeps them as members—team members rekindle their shared connection to the team. You'll want to bring the information into the room without spending a great deal of time on it. Typically, 15 minutes is plenty. We want to make the link, and move on.

Here's how to organize this time:

- First, participants quickly call out attractions.
- Next, the facilitator quickly reads the entire list out loud, as a brief review, and then asks people to reflect on what they've heard.

Call Out Attractions

You can trigger fast and furious reporting with the prompt:

"Let's start with your answers to the first question, by hearing what attracted you to this team, and what keeps you. Feel free to contribute your own reason or that of your partner. Just call them out, and we'll write them down as fast as we can."

With that you are off and running, and the flip chart sheet continues to fill until your hand begins to ache. Inevitably the list is delightful, like the reasons people fall in love.

Because things will move quickly, you need to be prepared to physically record the data. As mentioned above, I like to tape multiple sheets of flip chart paper to a blank wall in advance of the session. You can tape multiple sheets, one atop another, by just staggering the tape along the top. Then I position four or five sheets abreast.

This arrangement means that the group can see all the data we capture for each exercise at one time. When you are done with one exercise, you strip the top sheets and post them elsewhere in the room. Then, you're immediately ready to go on with four or five fresh sheets. If you use the standard flip chart easel, where you fold over an old page every time you start a new one, the group will lose visual access to the results of its work. That hinders the group's ability to stay with you as you move quickly through all this information. So find a flat wall and cover it with paper in advance of the session.

Reflect and Read the List Aloud

Although the process is moving fast, it's helpful to allow people a moment at this point to digest what they have created. Quickly read each item aloud to them once through, and then ask:

"Now that you've both heard and seen all these attractions to your team, what comments or reflections do you have?"

Participants typically say how much the items on the list share in common and how true they feel to them, even though most of the comments were generated by others. In just a few minutes, you rekindle the excitement that bonds people emotionally to the team.

When I'm leading a Grounded Visioning session, I sometimes take a moment at this point to mention that this list maps what you might call the core DNA of the team because it governs what draws people and keeps them. As such, it is a list of attributes that are well worth promoting and enhancing, so as to keep team membership a rewarding experience. And it is a good list of attributes to use in recruiting new people to the team because someone who wants the same things that drew everyone else to the team will probably be a good match.

Share Stories

The next point is to share some stories about high points of working with this team: times when participants felt most committed, most proud of the team, most engaged, connected, effective. This is the second question from the pairs' interviews. You should spend about 30 minutes on the stories.

Here is an overview of how you spend this time:

- First you ask for a few detailed stories describing their high points.
- Then you ask participants to identify common themes in the stories and call them out.

By sharing stories of high points, the group affirms what's best about the team and so maps how it is when it is at its very best. This creates the platform that allows us to dream big dreams without getting lost in generalities. Every story you are about to elicit and hear is true—it actually happened. Every theme you are about to surface derives from real experiences. Although our unabashedly positive orientation brings us quickly to some very heady stuff, all of it happened, and all of it is true. Thus any *vision* we then create is *grounded* in how we are when we are at our best.

Here's how you can introduce this topic:

> *Now we are going to hear your answers to the second question: stories about high points. It would be great to hear all of your stories, but unfortunately we don't have the time. So we'll have to screen them somehow. Here are the ones that we would most like to hear: the ones you so enjoyed telling, that you think the whole group would like to hear it, and the ones you so enjoyed hearing that you'll draft your partner to tell it, or tell it yourself. Who's got one for starters?*

People love to tell stories, and they love to hear them. There is never any short-age of people who want to share theirs with the group. In a small team, you may have time to hear them all. We'll assume that the group is big enough that you can only hear four or five.

As the stories are told, write out the major elements of the story in the words used by the speaker. It is important to use the speaker's words because that tells them they were truly heard and captures "the music" of the team in its own voice. Keep a running list that captures the story's key points.

When someone finishes telling his or her partner's story, ask the partner if he or she has anything to add. Often the telling of one story will trigger the telling of the next. Frequently, several people all chose to tell the same story as their high point. That tells you something, doesn't it? If so, let others elaborate on the main points mentioned by first storyteller before moving on.

Identify Themes

When you've heard four or five or six stories, more or less, enough to sense that you've invoked some essential truth about the team, it is time to pause and allow participants to digest what they have just revealed. You want them to notice common themes that run throughout the stories of how they are when they are at their very best.

To do this, quickly read aloud the key points of each story as you recorded them on the newsprint sheets. Next introduce a fresh sheet of paper that reads across the top: "When we are at our very best, we...," and ask team members to finish the sentence. What themes did they hear running through most, if not all, of the stories? They typically find many.

When this list is complete, read it aloud, so everyone can hear as well as see these remarkable testimonials to the team at its very best. These themes are always inspiring, yet every line is based on real people and events that actually happened. This is not blue-sky thinking. This is real. You are building the case for your team's ability to be great and do great things. Most people find it exhilarating.

A few find it unbearably uncomfortable. You may hear from them at this point. They say, "But this is not how we actually are, day to day. Normally we don't operate at this level. This is unrealistic. We're not talking about any of the things we don't do well."

You must be ready to intervene when this sentiment emerges. Your response is critical. Most of the team members, in their heart of hearts, want to follow you where you are taking them. They want to be great and to do great things. But, like everyone, they fear failure. People who second-guess at this point are voicing the fear that lurks in everyone's mind, that somehow we are all just fooling ourselves, and that it is time to get practical, and start solving problems!

Faced with this kind of very valid comment, here's what I typically say:

"You are right. We don't operate at this level day in and day out. That is the truth. But here's the thing. Most of us know that, and we live that sad truth all the time. What we don't do is acknowledge ourselves for how we are when we are at our very best. Yet that is also true."

To make the point it's helpful to draw a series of undulating lines across a page like a series of steep ocean waves, and then a straight line just below the peaks, and another straight line just above the troughs.

> *When we focus on problems, we are studying the troughs—how we are when we are not at our best. That is certainly true, but it doesn't give us much energy to go forward. When we focus on best practices, we are studying the peaks—how we are when we are at our best. That is also true, and yet it gives us energy to take on the real challenges we face. Both are true, but focusing on which one supports you to be your best? We are not asking you to avoid the truth, we are just asking you to acknowledge the truth about your team that supports you in being your best.*

These comments are usually sufficient to keep you on track. If not, ask for the critic's indulgence to follow the process to its conclusion, while reserving judgment until the end. I say something like this:

"Keep us honest. If you don't think by the end of this process that we're well positioned to do what matters, please let us know."

POST DREAMS, HOPES, AND ASPIRATIONS

Sharing attractions and stories and identifying themes have set the table for the feast. Now it is time to eat! After thinking about attractions and successes, people are well prepared to discuss dreams, hopes, and aspirations.

You'll use these dreams, hopes, and aspirations to craft your shared vision, so you should invest a good amount of your time on this third question from the pairs' interviews. Plan to spend about 30 minutes.

Here's how I introduce this topic:

"Now we would like to work with your answers to the third question—your three dreams, hopes, and aspirations for what this team might do or be. For us to work with this data, we're going to ask you to write each one of your three dreams, hopes, and aspirations individually on a separate adhesive note, using a marker."

Everyone should have a small stack of 3" by 5" adhesive notes and a single magic marker at this point. Although it seems obvious, I sometimes demonstrate how I want people to write their notes:

- Write only one dream, hope, or aspiration per note.
- Write on the note with it positioned in the horizontal or landscape orientation.
- Write large and legibly (up to about seven or eight words per note).
- Start with an action verb to give your hope some direction and clarity.
- Refer to your partner's notes if you need a reminder of what you said.

These brief instructions give us a better quality product when all the individual elements are assembled together.

When most people are finished writing, explain what happens next. Here's what I say:

Now we are going to share our dreams with each other and see what emerges. In a moment we're going to ask one of you to come forward and read your three dreams aloud, one at a time, and then post them anywhere on these large sheets of brown paper behind us on the wall. Your job as the first is the easiest, for you have a blank slate on which to post them. The next person who comes up, after reading his or hers aloud too, also posts them on the sheets. But if any of these are similar to ones already posted, the person should show that by posting them physically together, in a small cluster. Got it? Who wants to go first?

Watch Ideas Converge

In so saying we engage our participants in a simple yet powerful process inspired by a quality management tool known as "affinity diagramming" (for more information on the history of this method, see Chapter 14, "The Spark of Sight").

By asking individuals to stand, walk to the front of the room, and read aloud their dreams, hopes, and aspirations for the team, we are asking them to take a risk, express themselves, and assume ownership of their hopes, even as they surrender them to the emerging vision on the wall. This goes quickly and most people are happy to participate in this way.

It is somewhat disorienting to leave your seat in the room and come up close to the wall, so people often lose sight of where their contribution fits with the others posted on the wall. It's helpful for you as facilitator to stay oriented to the emerging clusters so you can quickly propose a location for the note, should it be proffered helplessly in your direction. I use large sheets of brown kraft or butcher paper, typically three sheets each about four feet by four feet, posted on a flat wall, to allow plenty of space to capture the notes.

Once the last notes are read, and you've checked that no one else has any others, you are ready to do a final sort of the emerging clusters. At this point someone usually asks if we have invested in 3M—the wall is a virtual blizzard of adhesive notes, hugging tightly together in little groups.

Label Ideas

Most of the sorting of the emerging themes in your shared vision has already been done, very organically, one item at a time. Yet important work remains. There may be elements that ended in one cluster that best belong in another. There may be stand-alone items that, upon reflection, belong with a group that emerged later.

In addition, you can bring the emergent clusters into sharper relief by giving them titles. Beginning with a cluster of notes, read each aloud (partly to refresh everyone's memories, partly to help people in the back of the room who can't read them, and partly to invoke them once again into the space) and ask: "Do all these still belong together?" If not, you need to find a better home for that idea. If different participants have different opinions, locate the author and let him or her have the final say, so we can keep moving. If these dreams do belong together, I ask:

"What few words would capture the essence of what is being conveyed by these ideas?"

Figure 6.1
The picture emerges: Cluster ideas and label them to highlight elements of the shared vision.

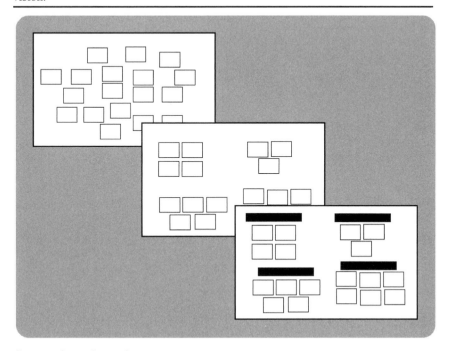

Illustration by Cindy Murphy.

Participants will offer various suggestions. You should repeat them to the group to get a sense of which one wins the most support. Finding that one, write the title on an adhesive note of a different, brighter color so that it stands out when you post it on top of the cluster. Continue this process until every note has found a home cluster, and every cluster has a header.

This is a good time to step back. I often find myself saying something like:

"This process is like watching a photograph emerge from a chemical bath, and none of us knows what it looks like until we're done. Now we can see it clearly—a picture of our shared dreams, hopes, and aspirations."

Then I read aloud only the headers to highlight the major elements of the emerging shared vision. This is a good time to ask:

"What comments or reflections do you have based on what you've seen and heard?"

Engage Many Senses

Note that it is often helpful to use language invoking more than one sense modality—such as seeing and hearing. This is because some people primarily process information visually, while others do so aurally. Using both verbs engages both types of learners in a subconscious way.

The predominant emotion at this point is often amazement. Many people, if not most, enter a Grounded Visioning session convinced that little common ground exists within the diverse gathering that has been assembled. They warn me up front by saying things like "You will really have to earn your pay with this group" or "We don't envy you being in your position," that kind of thing. They are skeptical about the process, its speed, and its promised results. At this point they are often delighted—and surprised—at what is happening.

In some cases, a participant will comment that the titles on the wall are not all conceptually equal. Some are goals, some are tactics, etc. At a Grounded Visioning session, facilitators do not explicitly define what they are looking for, in terms of formal goal language, so that isn't necessarily a problem. We are looking for dreams, hopes, and aspirations, and they take many forms. For most people, the emotion and meaning conveyed by the words is more potent than the actual wording. In some situations, I do help the planners to apply a planning hierarchy of some kind, after the fact, to organize the results. If you are uncomfortable with this kind of ambiguity, you should probably give people a short training up front on how to write elegant goals, and ask the participants to express their dreams, hopes, and aspirations in that format.[2]

CHOOSE PRIORITIES

As you review the emerging vision with the team with a mind to implementation, you can get lucky. Sometimes an entire roomful of people will reveal a shared passion for only three major things. In such cases, it is fair to ask the group if they have the resources to pursue all three at once. They very well may. If so, no further prioritization is necessary.

In other instances, a more dazzling array of possibilities will have emerged. It is hard to tell, at a glance, where the true passion of the team is heading. You will know that every item is important to one or more members of the team, but the team as a whole doesn't yet have a shared sense of priorities. In these instances, operating in a short amount of time, you will need to resort to multi-voting.

In multi-voting, everyone gets a number of adhesive dots to use in expressing preference for one dream or another. The facilitator draws a target circle by each of the titles on the emerging vision. The usual formula for distributing dots divides the total number of choices by three. For example, a person choosing among nine choices would receive three dots. I advise people to limit their voting to one dot per target and "share the wealth," so they do not put all of their dots in any one area. That would distort the results.

You should again read aloud the headers so that everyone knows the choices. Next, ask everyone to make choices in their seats and to signal that they have chosen by giving us the universal "thumbs up" sign. Eventually, everyone's thumb is in the air. At this point, I call out:

"Place your dots!"

Everyone Votes Simultaneously

This brings everyone up out of their chairs at once. The ensuing rush to the wall preserves some measure of anonymity (as to who voted for what) and creates a playful effect.

Sometimes I give people three dots of three different colors. I assign a different point value to each color, for example, green equals three points, blue, two, and red, one. This way, everyone picks his or her top three choices in rank order. The dots are tallied, with their weighted point values counted. When the votes are in, I quickly tally them and read off the scores. Using a weighting strategy is more complicated, but it gives you more information.

Think of multi-voting not so much as a team making decisions but as a team clarifying its preferences. It is certainly not achieving consensus. Surprisingly, for most groups, operating under tight time frames, multi-voting is good enough. It is fast, and the results are usually compelling. They are visually obvious in an instant. The essential elements of a shared vision emerge for all to see. Typically, the vast majority or participants favor a very limited set of actions. These preferred dreams are immediately identifiable, often before we count the dots.

Sometimes at this point, I will quickly test for consensus, just in case it is easily within our grasp. I might say,

"It seems that the emerging sense of the team is to move forward in these three areas: x, y, and z. Is there any objection to these being the team's main course of action going forward?"

Table 6.2
Action Planning Template

Task	Person responsible	Time frame

If there are no objections, I would note consensus and move on to next steps. If objections are raised, they can be noted and worked out in next steps.

PLAN NEXT STEPS

Perhaps you have already planned next steps for the team. At this point, you would revisit them to see if they are still appropriate. Perhaps the meeting planners had agreed in advance that the top three priorities of the team would form the basis for work groups, which now can be organized around the actual priorities. If so, you might ask for volunteers and group leaders. Perhaps the meeting planners had decided to just see where things stood at the end of the Grounded Visioning session and then decide what needs to happen next, on the spot. If so I might ask,

"What has to happen next to ensure that all the value that comes out of today gets captured, and put to use?"

We use a classic action planning template (Table 6.2) to record the team's commitments.

At this point, it is good to remind people that those who step forward as leaders of an initiative don't have to do all the work. They just have to make sure it gets done. I call this role the MAP, or Most Accountable Person. The group can quickly build an action plan.

Just as you run out of time, ask people to call out some of the reasons for optimism they heard earlier, that the team's hopes might actually be realized. With that chorus of encouragement, the session draws to a close.

NOTES

1. David Sibbet and Allan Drexler, *Team Performance Principles/Practices* (San Francisco: The Grove Consultants International, 1994), 75.

2. For example, see online guides to SMART goals (specific, measurable, attainable, realistic, timely) such as http://www.uncommon-knowledge.co.uk/goal_setting/smart _4.html (accessed May 27, 2008) or http://www.topachievement.com/smart.html (accessed May 27, 2008).

7

Case Studies: Grounded Visioning for Small Groups

The whole group works together, assisted by one facilitator.

Never doubt that a small group of thoughtful, committed citizens can change the world. Indeed, it is the only thing that ever has.

—Margaret Mead

L et's take a look at the small group method in action. This chapter presents two case studies:

- How the volunteer board of a community farm mapped new goals after achieving satisfying successes.
- How a downtown improvement group of 40 people identified top priorities for positive change.

For the community farm, everyone could work together around one table. For the downtown revitalization effort, the group was on the large side, but the meeting leader still used the "small group" method successfully. That is, the whole group worked together; there was no breakdown into table groups.

This is the key distinction between the small group and the large group methods. For small groups, the meeting facilitator serves as the leader of the entire process. The leader explains every task and does not enlist volunteer facilitators. Interviews take place in pairs (not through stories shared in small groups). After the participants work in pairs, the whole group works as one, guided by the facilitator.

This format works well when the number of participants is small enough. When you have a larger group, as with the downtown improvement group, you have to keep the sharing moving right along and you might want to allow a bit more time. It takes more facilitation experience, but it can be done.

Grounded Visioning Gets Results

Organization: Community Organic Farm
Planning need: Reset growth goals in aftermath of success
Result: New goals, new focus for decision-making

Organization: Downtown Center Associates
Planning need: Desire to contribute to town planning
Result: New priorities for downtown improvement

As you are reading these cases, think about the choices these groups made, and how they might relate to choices you would make about your own team. For example:

- Both these groups chose the small group version of the Grounded Visioning method. Which version would be best for your team?
- The community organic farm came to visioning with the momentum of recent past success. Does your team have past success powering it from behind, like wind in your sails, or do you need to jump-start your team?
- The farm's volunteer board used the visioning process to define a cherished set of values, based on deeply held beliefs, to guide their decision-making. Does your team have a powerful set of guiding ideas?
- The downtown improvement group came to visioning with an open invitation to its many allies to help chart its future. Which allies have a stake in the future success of your team?
- The downtown improvement group used the visioning process to define common goals that businesses, some of whom compete with each other, could agree to pursue together. What larger, shared goals might unite you with those with whom you compete?

COMMUNITY ORGANIC FARM: HOW TO GROW WITHOUT RISKING THE CORE?

A wonderful community organic farm grows more than 25,000 pounds of fresh organic produce each year with the help of thousands of community volunteers. The farm donates all of the produce to area meal programs, food pantries, and shelters. The volunteers farm a 10-acre parcel on public land that has been continuously cultivated for more than 300 years and features an educational pavilion and greenhouse. The organization had recently transitioned, successfully, from being founder-led to being managed by a diverse working board, all volunteers, with a paid part-time administrator and a paid seasonal farmer. Nearly 2,000 volunteers per season, of all ages and abilities, supply all additional needed labor on the farm. During the winter, volunteers bring educational outreach programs about food and organic agriculture into area public schools.

This is clearly a successful organization. When the organization approached me to help create a new five-year strategic plan, it had already accomplished a great deal in its first dozen years. The members had, in their own words:

- Grown more than 200,000 pounds of organic produce for hunger relief.
- Supported dozens of area hunger-relief organizations—and established a local hunger relief program of their own.
- Inspired thousands of community volunteers.
- Created a stable organization and governing structure.
- Established an innovative organic farm (fields, pavilion, greenhouse) that serves as a stable, safe, handicapped-accessible, and dynamic base for the group's work.
- Reached out to local schools, faith communities, businesses, and others—building awareness of the farm and the group's work.
- Created an atmosphere of openness that attracts a diverse community of volunteers and supporters at all levels (board, financial supporters, partners, others).
- Fostered creativity (and a sense of humor) among the farm staff, volunteers, and board.
- Provided flexible, meaningful volunteer opportunities tailored to the needs of a wide range of individuals and groups—including people of all ages and backgrounds, as well as people with disabilities.

What's Next for a Thriving Nonprofit?

This modest organization, with an annual budget under $130,000, had chosen to grow slowly, deliberately, and sustainably. "At year 12 we were at a critical juncture," said the board chairperson. "We didn't face a pressing problem. We didn't need a rescue or a turnaround. It was more of the subtle problem of a thriving nonprofit: How do we direct our considerable energies toward achievable goals?"

He added, "We are a very matter-of-fact group. We needed to do something that was simple, fast, and not a lot of process. It had to have all three or there would be trouble."

The board and staff agreed to a three-quarter-day visioning retreat featuring three core components:

- **Values.** A conversation on values drawn from attractions data and high point stories from the brief appreciative interviews.
- **Vision.** A conversation on vision drawn from shared dreams, hopes, and aspirations from the brief appreciative interviews.
- **Goals.** A conversation on goals drawn from the aggregate vision.

After the initial appreciative interviews, each of the three conversations lasted from 60 to 90 minutes.

Volunteers and Staff Identify Core Values

The conversation on values unearthed a set of compelling and distinctive beliefs that were both widely and deeply shared by members of board and staff. In summary, they came to understand their enduring values as:

- **Integrity.** We remain true to our mission. We work hard to grow high-quality produce, serve the needs of our recipients, provide an exceptional experience to each volunteer, and maximize the generous support of our donors.
- **Free.** We donate all of our food for free. We give our produce to hunger relief organizations—and directly to people in need—always for free. This approach keeps our operation simple and enables us to give recipients the best possible produce.
- **Openness.** We are accessible to everyone. We welcome volunteers of all ages and from all backgrounds, and work to reach out to underserved groups in our community. Our board and staff also rely on diverse strengths and perspectives.
- **Experience.** We nurture joy and wonder in our garden. We create compelling, meaningful volunteer opportunities tailored to the unique needs of every individual —always provided for free.
- **Scale.** We respect the power of small. Working well with small groups fosters the personal contact and nurturing community at our core. Our farming is also on a small scale, enabling a closer connection with the land.
- **Sustainability.** We grow in a careful, considered fashion.

Aspirations Cluster around Three Themes

The conversation on vision gave rise to eight distinct aspirations, which clustered into three main goals. After the posting and sorting, this picture of dreams, hopes, and aspirations emerged with startling clarity:

- **Grow organic produce.** Manage our farm, secure our land.
- **Grow community.** Create an engaging, meaningful volunteer experience, educate and reach out, serve as a model for hunger relief and volunteerism.
- **Strengthen the organization.** Raise the funds necessary to accomplish our goals, strengthen the organization financially, attract talented, committed people to our organization.

For the final conversation on goals, the participants organized themselves in two rounds of work groups to sketch out, for each goal, these three deliverables:

- Identify persons responsible for managing and achieving this goal.
- Identify near-term objectives for the coming year in support of this goal.
- Identify long-term objectives in the ensuring years in support of this goal.

Strategic Plan Makes It Possible to Focus and Say No

Based on the work of these six hours and the follow-up by each work group, the board chairperson produced a 26-page, five-year strategic plan. "That plan doesn't sit on a shelf—it's a working document," he reflected, a year later. The board chairperson continued:

> Nonprofits have a tendency to do the same thing over and over again. This made us look for incremental ways to increase the numbers we serve, and increase what we do, without risking the core. The plan set the stage for a major leadership transition, without a problem; a major upgrade in staff; the addition of a full extra day per week of service, and an exponential increase in our volunteers. That day worked for us in so many ways.
>
> Nonprofits run on volunteers. The level of enthusiasm you generate is key. People left that session feeling confident, and ready to move ahead. It propels you forward faster. It has been wonderful.
>
> Our values haven't changed a bit. Those values are the first thing we show people. We use them in every presentation. They give us a litmus test to gauge every new initiative. They are always there—on deep background. Take the one that we're not selling anything. It is not an option. It is decided. A lot of what you do as a leader is deflect ideas that aren't on mission. Values give you an impartial measuring stick. It takes two points to make a line, and three to enclose a space. Our three points— values, mission, and goals—give us clear direction. It's almost impossible to do something stupid.

DOWNTOWN CENTER ASSOCIATES: GRANTS PROMPT REASSESSMENT FOR COMMUNITY ORGANIZATION

New England is full of beautiful, historic cities and towns. Many of these downtowns have aged and lost vitality as changing settlement and transportation patterns took people, money, and commerce to the suburbs. The most dynamic downtowns fought back, winning back consumers and residents through targeted economic revitalization programs that highlighted the convenience, character, and joy of living and working in a vibrant downtown.

One city outside Greater Boston organized a group I'll call Downtown Center Associates. This organization brought together property owners, retail and office people, concerned neighbors, town officials, nonprofits, and corporations committed to making their downtown a vital, exciting place. Over 40 years, this all-volunteer organization set a great example of a public/private partnership, supporting town ventures and initiating private ones in support of its downtown as a good place to live, work, or visit.

Downtown Center Associates at a Crossroads

By the mid-1990s more than 70 downtown businesses were active members. By the late 1990s, Downtown Center Associates received three significant down-town revitalization grants from the Commonwealth of Massachusetts. These funds enabled the organization to hire its first professional planner to serve as executive director and downtown manager. At this point, the planner approached me about holding a visioning session for the downtown.

The situation was complex. The town had already completed an open space plan. The town planner had hopes of initiating a comprehensive master plan soon, including sections featuring open space, downtown, economic development, land use, zoning, infrastructure/public facilities/technology, housing, and transportation. The Associates were eager to move forward with planning. They didn't want to duplicate the work of the town or alienate it by assuming its role, but they also didn't want to sit by idly and do nothing, in case the town was not able to get going on such a major task.

Town government and the volunteers reached an agreement in a series of public-private conversations. Town and volunteers would collaborate on a joint process. The Downtown Center Associates would initiate a Grounded Visioning process focusing exclusively on the downtown, but using the core framework of the town's master planning process as its guide. This process would complement the planning work of the town, thus contributing significantly to the town's downtown planning component. In effect, the Downtown Center Associates would jump-start the town's process, and the town would build on the work done by the Associates. A joint memorandum of understanding confirmed these points.

Two Hours to a Downtown Vision

With the can-do mentality of an organization driven by business people, the Associates set a date for a community visioning session straight away and limited it to two hours. They picked a widely accessible location—the community library—and time—from 5:30 to 7:30 p.m. The Associates hoped to attract about 20 community leaders.

My task was to help everyone who showed up to create a shared vision for their downtown in two hours or less. In addition, the meeting planners wanted to promote a positive connection with and commitment to the work of the Associates, to engage and identify new leaders, to generate a list of concrete improvement goals for the downtown, to set priorities among those goals, and to be clear about next steps. Table 7.1 shows our two-hour agenda.

Table 7.1
Two-Hour Grounded Visioning Session
Downtown Center Associates

Time (minutes)	Task
20	Welcome, overview, explain task
20	Appreciative interviews (attractions, high points, dreams)
10	Share attractions briefly
10	Share high point stories briefly
30	Post and sort dreams, hopes, and aspirations
15	Set priorities by multi-voting and review results
15	Review next steps

We decided to design and lead the evening using the small group method because we really had no idea how many people might show up. The group had the services of a professional facilitator, so that was not an issue. We didn't know who was coming and therefore couldn't preplan diverse work group assignments. The library wasn't equipped to offer lots of round tables. And the business people in the planning group wanted the transparency of seeing and hearing everyone. So the thinking was that it would make sense to stay together as a large group, move quickly, and hear from as many people as time would permit.

That night, 40 people filled the library community room. One wall was covered with large sheets of brown paper to hold the posted dreams and aspirations. Aside from setting out refreshments, that was all we did in advance. After a welcome by the sponsor and an overview of the evening by the facilitator, the appreciative interviewing task was explained. Pairs quickly formed and the room filled with the pleasant animated sound of engaged people talking.

Love of Downtown Inspires Dreams

Participants shared some of the qualities that attracted them to this downtown and keep them living and working in it. Some of the highlights included:

Figure 7.1
The core of Grounded Visioning: In pairs, people share high points and dreams.

Illustration by Cindy Murphy.

revitalization, the common and green spaces, churches and historic buildings, the sense of community and family, the feel of a small New England town with a touch of the city.

Participants shared stories of high points in their experience of this downtown, with themes like: the exciting success of a recent public-private street revitalization effort; the successful building of a new, and tastefully designed, municipal complex; the introduction of new art work at the train station; an experience of night life, community events, spirit, and lively street traffic.

The pump was primed, and it was time for everyone to share his or her aspirations. One by one, each participant came to the front of the room to announce and post his or her hopes. A shared picture of the future of this revitalized downtown slowly took shape. Nineteen discrete aspirations were posted; participants quickly grouped them into five major themes. The multi-voting quickly led to six major recommendations.

The five themes and the six recommendations emerged in those two hours:

- **Transportation.** Increase parking.
- **Economic development and new technology.** Build arts and entertainment identity downtown, continue restoration and rehabilitation work on buildings.
- **Land use and open space.** Preserve existing open space.
- **Housing.** Create new housing of various types—affordable, senior, mixed use, etc.
- **Infrastructure and public facilities.** Underground utilities.

One of these recommendations—increased parking—was informally made by acclamation, prior to the multi-voting. In sharing reactions to the sorted themes, it became obvious that that need was universally felt by everyone in the room.

Collaborative Vision Leads to Housing that Revitalizes Downtown

The 40 participants loved the visioning process. It was fast, engaging, and productive. The business sponsors were proud to have hosted something so efficient. The session quickly captured the essence of what most people in town were feeling without requiring an extensive, expensive, time-consuming process. The priorities formed the basis of a presentation to a future—and even larger—community meeting. The results eventually fed the downtown portion of the town's five-year master plan. The Federal Home Loan Bank's award for community development for that year went to the Downtown Center Associates.

The acclaimed goal—more parking—became the Associates' top priority, albeit an intractable one. The Associates embarked upon a real estate feasibility analysis that evaluated alternative land use and financing scenarios for parking and mixed-use development in the downtown. Bolstered by this analysis, the Associates set out to obtain grant funds for further study of the identified alternatives.

The housing priority led to learning initiatives related to smart growth principles that provide a logic and framework for increasing density around transportation hubs and walking centers. This learning led to two evening design workshops at which residents applied smart growth principles to their actual downtown. The excitement created by this event led to innovative new zoning laws featuring high-density, mixed-use downtown housing. These laws led to four exciting new developments—and counting. Said a member of the town's planning board, "The people who live there will be more reliant on trains and public transportation. They'll be close to places to eat downtown, and this development will create a more attractive downtown."

—— 8 ——

Step-by-Step: Grounded Visioning
for Large Groups

With larger groups, participants take on some of the facilitator's tasks.

The more you lose yourself in something bigger than yourself, the more energy you will have.

—Norman Vincent Peale[1]

One of the tremendously exciting qualities of Grounded Visioning is that, with minor modifications, it scales very well to groups as large as 250. This gives organizations a tremendous freedom to think very seriously, perhaps for the first time in their history, about who should be in the room for the Grounded Visioning conversation. Discussions that had been limited in the past, consciously or unconsciously, to a convenient size for the planning process can be freed of that constraint. Organizations can think creatively—and courageously—about the full range of stakeholders who are committed to the future of the organization. Everyone gets a seat at the table.

For groups between 25 and 250, the underlying Grounded Visioning process is essentially the same. But you'll need to adjust the mechanics to accommodate larger numbers. Here are some of the differences:

- You divide the whole group into small groups of 6 to 10 (typically 8) that work through the tasks of the Grounded Visioning process. There can be as many as 30 groups or more working together in parallel. The process allows for them to aggregate all their good work into a coherent whole within the time allowed.
- Because working with more people takes more time—even getting everyone into a seat takes longer—you typically need to pare down the interview process from four questions to just two questions: stories about high points and dreams for the future.

Table 8.1
Schedule for a Large Group Grounded Visioning Session
Six Steps, Tailored to Large Groups

Time (minutes)	Task
30	Gathering
15	*Assemble your stakeholders:* Welcome, orient, and explain task
25	*Ignite your spark:* Introduce selves and share stories
40	*Share best practices:* Identify themes and when your organization is at its best; share themes with whole group
15	Break
40	*Share your dreams:* Share in pairs; share and cluster at tables
50	*Select the best:* Post, sort, and prioritize
25	*Plan next steps:* Explain next steps; share appreciations

- You need to arrange the meeting space carefully so that there is plenty of space for everyone and plenty of wall space to accommodate the outputs from the many work groups.
- Volunteers at each table must take on more of the facilitator's role.
- You should use handouts and worksheets (samples are in Appendices) that help people at the tables succeed in taking on the facilitator's role.

Using the small work group as a building block, one or two facilitators are able to work with numbers of participants ranging from 25 to 250 and still create a shared vision within the tight time frame of a half day or less.

Table 8.1 shows the basic schedule for a four-hour large group process suitable for groups of 25 to 250.

GATHERING

During the gathering period, participants enter the space, receive their participant materials, and find their assigned tables. You should include this time in the agenda because it sets the expectation of an arrival time that is well in advance of the actual start time, thus ensuring a real, on-time start. Large groups of people need lots of transaction time to get from one place to another. As long as there is plenty of hot coffee and tea to drink, refreshments to enjoy, and people to meet, no one seems to mind being drawn in to the meeting room well before the last possible minute. Planning for gathering time creates a crisp, high-quality start.

In addition, you can use this gathering time to set a relaxed, creative, and productive mood. For example, you could run a slide show with pictures of your colleagues and the results of their good work. You could play recorded music as people arrive or even arrange for a small performance of live music if the arts are integral to the organization.

During the gathering time, participants find their way to tables to which they have been, typically, preassigned. Usually the tables have numbers on them, or perhaps colors, that differentiate one from another. You should mark this code on participants' name tags. That way, Jane Doe learns when she registers that she is assigned to sit at table 6. Her name tag has the number six on it in case she forgets.

If the crowd is particularly sensitive to being told what to do and where to sit, we coach the registration team members to give a standard explanation, something like,

"We assign people from diverse backgrounds to tables in advance to ensure a maximum diversity of views in every conversation."

If the crowd is especially sensitive or particularly large, and time is especially short, we provide a written explanation with the name tag. Usually, assigned seating is not a problem. Still, it's polite to explain it and thank people for their flexibility in your opening remarks.

ASSEMBLE YOUR STAKEHOLDERS

Just like the small group process, the large group event typically begins with a warm welcome by the sponsor. This is a good time to share your hopes for the session. People are in their seats, ready to work. You should keep your remarks brief and upbeat.

Most large group processes draw together people with diverse stakes in the success of the sponsoring organization or community. This is the time to recognize these stakeholder groups, one at a time, and to ask individuals who see themselves as affiliated with these groups to stand, as a group, and be acknowledged briefly with applause. Some individuals will stand more than once, which is fine. This is a great way to show participants, quickly and visually, just who is in the room. This simple act both celebrates the diversity in the room and validates the inclusive foundation of the eventual Grounded Vision, soon to emerge.

Then, the facilitators frame the session. Typically, I present a brief summary of how this meeting is different from typical meetings (see "Set the Tone for Your Grounded Visioning Session"). I say,

We have worked hard to bring together what we call "the whole system" in this room, and at every table. This ensures the fullest possible diversity of views is present at every table, in every discussion. By listening to each other, we see the world differently, and from that insight develop more creative, integrative ideas. The only way one or two of us can run such a large meeting successfully is with lots of help. So we will ask each of you, at your table work groups, to self-manage your work. We've broken the jobs done into a few simple roles, and that makes it easy for everyone to do a small part, and thus make us all more effective. Our meeting is designed to build a common database together, so that we all have access to the same information about our hopes and dreams. We don't have any experts who will come in and speak at you. We trust that everything we need to know is within this

---

Set the Tone for Your Grounded Visioning Session

Sample Handout for a Large Group

How this meeting differs from typical meetings:

- The *whole system* participates. We invite a cross section of as many interested parties as is practical. This means more diversity and less hierarchy than usual in working meeting, and it gives each person a chance to be heard and to learn other ways of looking at the task at hand.
- Participants *self-manage* their work. We ask you to take responsibility for your work in small groups—for facilitating, recording, timekeeping, reporting, and managing your data. That means helping each other be productive and taking responsibility for your perceptions and actions.
- Participants build a *common database* together. We develop shared understandings together based on our own experience and reflection, not the determinations of experts. We trust each other to know what is best for our institution. We trust ourselves to risk seeing the world through the eyes of others.
- Participants seek to find *shared ground*, rather than manage conflict. We engage in *dialogue*, not problem-solving, as our main means of communicating. That means honoring our differences rather than having to reconcile them.

Source: Adapted from Marvin R. Weisbord and Sandra Janoff, *Future Search: An Action Guide to Finding Common Ground in Organizations & Communities* (San Francisco: Berrett-Koehler, 1995), 179.

---

community, and that as we share it, we can make good choices together. It is our intention to find common ground here today. We don't have time to solve all the problems that there may be to solve, and that is not our intention. Rather it is to foster dialogue between us, so that the common ground we share can emerge.

Keep the Process Simple

We then present our OARRs—outcomes, agenda, roles, and rules—generally as described in Chapter 6. For a large group meeting, I use handouts, so everyone has the same information about the agenda, roles, and ground rules. Sample handouts are reproduced in Appendices.

On the agenda handout, you should include the following information:

- Facilitators' names and bios.
- Purpose of the Grounded Visioning session, for example, "to define a shared vision and direction for our organization."
- Desired outcomes, for example, share what's best about our organization in a fun and positive way; create a shared vision for the future; set key goals for our organization's desired achievements in the next two to three years; set up goal teams for action planning as part of a strategic plan; create action plan for next steps.

- Tasks to be accomplished and times for each activity, including breaks. For a large group, you can summarize the three main tasks as "share high point stories about our organization," "create shared vision for our organization's desired achievements in next two to three years," and "next steps/action plans."

Keep the handouts short. The tasks look easier when the descriptions are short and sweet. And, in fact, they are easy.

Explain Overall Roles

It's also good to remind participants of their overall responsibilities:

- Provide information and make meaning.
- Manage own small groups.
- Develop vision and commit to it.
- Engage in actions to make vision real.

For a large group, I usually hand out a written list of the facilitator's responsibilities, so everyone knows what to expect:

- Set time and tasks.
- Facilitate large group discussions.
- Keep purpose front and center.
- Assist in follow-through.

Explain Ground Rules

I typically introduce ground rules that include some aspects unique to the large group setting. I might say something like the following:

"Remember that everyone's ideas are valid from their point of view and deserve to be heard. If you make room for the airing of the ideas of others, they will make room for the airing of ideas of your own. We ask you all to listen to understand, not to judge. Too often we confine our listening to gathering evidence to refute what someone else is saying. It is wiser to do as Stephen Covey advises, 'Seek first to understand, then to be understood.' We don't have time to work all the differences that may come up in such a diverse room. So we ask you instead to just acknowledge them, and keep moving on toward finding common ground and seeking joint action."

For large groups, I frequently include these ground rules on a handout:[2]

- Remember: All ideas are valid.
- Listen to understand, not judge.
- Acknowledge differences, but don't "work" them.
- Write everything on flip charts.
- Observe time frames for tasks.
- Seek common ground and joint action.
- Have fun while getting lots done!

That way, people have a constant reminder when they are working independently of the facilitator.

Don't be shy about making this plea:

"Write everything on flip charts. If something important gets said, and not written down, it's like the proverbial tree falling alone in the forest. Did it make a sound? Did that important voice get heard?"

We always have people write their work on flip chart pad pages, rather than keying in to computers, because the notes give the whole work group a shared visual record of their conversations and conclusions. Recently clients have found it cheaper and easier to buy small tabletop easel pads (with self-adhesive pages) than to find or rent the larger, freestanding easels. Either will work, but the smaller, tabletop versions seem less intimidating to recorders.

As the room's official taskmaster, you should remind everyone,

"Please observe time frames for individual tasks. That is how we will get so much done and still have you by our promised ending time. We thank you for that."

Keep in mind that it is important to be encouraging. You might say something like,

"Working with good people on things we really care about is fun. So by all means, feel free to have fun while getting lots done!"

Now, we are ready to begin. At this time, I typically don't take questions. We just move on.

LARGE GROUP PARTICIPANTS TAKE ON LEADERSHIP ROLES

As in the small group process, the facilitator now proceeds to explain the first task. But the dynamics of large groups impose different requirements on the participants. In order for one or two facilitators to work successfully with hundreds of people, the members of the table work groups must manage themselves. For each table, participants must fill five leadership roles:[3]

- *Facilitator:* Keeps the group on task and ensures that everyone gets heard.
- *Timekeeper:* Keeps the group aware of how much time is left. The timekeeper does not just say, "Time's up!" The timekeeper lets the group know how much time is left all during the discussion, not just two or three minutes before the end.
- *Recorder:* Legibly records the group's main points using the words of participants.
- *Reporter:* Shares the table group's results with the whole group.
- *Data manager:* Makes sure every post gets labeled and no information is lost.

Again, I use a short handout to summarize these roles. You can see a sample in Appendix 7.

To get started, I might say,

"Please take 60 seconds right now to assign your roles. Traditionally we say that the timekeeper is the person with the biggest watch, so you might start there. Sixty seconds! Five roles! Go!"

I wait while the table work groups pick people to play these roles, so I know that roles get assigned and they get assigned quickly. After a minute, I say,

"Can I see the hands in the air of the facilitators at every table?"

Wait until you see at least one hand from every table. That way if the group has not yet assigned the other roles, you at least have identified a person who will make sure this happens.

TIME-SAVING STRATEGIES FOR LARGE GROUPS

For large groups, just like for small groups, appreciative interviewing is how we gather the stories and inspirations that power the Grounded Visioning session.

For large groups, I often reduce the interview questions from four to two. I drop the "attractions" question (What attracted you to this team and keeps you involved?). Given time it takes for a large group to move from one question to the next, we don't always have the time to work in it. For the same reasons, I drop the "reasons for optimism" question (Name one reason for optimism that these dreams can come true.).

In my experience, the core questions of the appreciative interview are the "high points" and the "dreams, hopes, and aspirations" questions:

- **High points.** In your experience of this team, think of a time when you felt most committed, most proud to be part of it, most engaged, most alive and connected. Tell that story and what made it so great.
- **Dreams, hopes, and aspirations.** Imagine a positive future for this team. What are three dreams, hopes, or aspirations that you have for what this team might do or be?

If you have to cut corners because of limited time, these are the two questions to keep.

SHARE BEST PRACTICES

Now that we have addressed some of the logistics of dealing with larger groups, it is time to get down to the core tasks of Grounded Visioning, beginning with appreciative interviewing (as described in chapters 2 and 6 and summarized in Appendix 8).

To keep large groups on track, I divide the time for sharing high points as follows:

- 20 minutes: Table group members share stories and high points (Appendix 8).
- 20 minutes: Groups identify common themes and develop statements of belief: "When we are at our best, we..." (Appendix 9).
- 15–25 minutes: Report and share stories with the larger group (the amount of time will vary, depending on the number of tables you have to report, allowing about a minute or so per report).

And I distribute a worksheet describing each of these steps, so people can easily refresh their memories. You can see samples of these worksheets in Appendices.

Share Stories

I start by explaining the appreciative task. I ask people to introduce themselves by name and to share a story of a high point in their experience with the sponsoring business, organization, or community. This task does double duty, functioning both as an icebreaker and as a data gathering device.

We give the table groups 20 minutes, or about two minutes per person for an eight person table, to share high points. People introduce themselves and tell about a time they felt connected, proud, engaged, inspired.

During this activity, the *facilitator* makes sure that each person has a turn. *Timekeepers* alert speakers when their time is up. *Recorders* take notes.

You will find that people enjoy this activity and that you need to interrupt the hubbub to explain the next activity. When it is time to finish, I often use a brass temple bell to capture people's attention. The bell cuts through sound effectively, even in a tremendously noisy environment, and is more pleasant than shouting. A firm voice over a microphone works well too.

Figure 8.1
Members of large groups manage the Grounded Visioning: At each table, participants take on roles of facilitator, recorder, timekeeper, and so on.

Illustration by Cindy Murphy.

Identify Common Themes

Next, I ask participants to identify the common themes they heard in the stories just told, making a list as they go. *Facilitators* ask the question:

"*What are the common themes in our stories?*"

Recorders write the themes on a flip chart.

Based on these themes, I ask the groups to assert some beliefs about how they (as a business, organization, or community) are when they are at their best. *Facilitators* ask the group to complete the sentence:

"*When our organization is at its best, we . . .*"

I am looking for just one or two examples—just the highlights. I give them 20 minutes, more than enough time. *Recorders* write down the belief statements. *Data managers* post the flip charts so the large group can see them.

To help with time management, you can subdivide this time: 10 minutes to identify common themes and 10 minutes to decide on some beliefs.

Report

After 20 minutes, the work groups are ready to make their first reports. They have shared their stories and felt the excitement that bubbles up in an appreciative review of high points. They have translated those highly specific stories into common themes and then into belief statements. *Reporters* are ready to stand and proclaim how they are when they are at their very best.

The energy in the room, already positive from the start of the storytelling, gets hiked up a notch. Every table report makes an impact on the whole group, like a log thrown on an energy bonfire that is building in the center of the room. That fire feeds on the unabashedly positive sentiments being proclaimed (all of which, mind you, are based on real people and events).

To keep things moving, I ask for very brief reports—one minute or less. You can do three things to help people who are otherwise unpracticed speakers to routinely accomplish these crisp reports:

- Set a clear expectation that reports will be short, to the point, in a minute or less. Companies pay millions of dollars for a 60-second ad for the Super Bowl. A great deal of information can be conveyed in very little time. Remind your reporters to "Think Super Bowl ads!"
- Design the task so that the group's output is limited to just one or two structured belief statements. Do not encourage reporters to offer a review of all stories told, all common themes revealed, all beliefs articulated, etc. That would take much more time; don't allow it.
- Put small bottles of children's bubble liquid on each table. Tell the *timekeepers* to blow bubbles gently at their *reporters* if they go beyond a minute. In this way, you can delegate the task of time enforcement and turn what might have been a struggle for the mike into a reason for the whole group to dissolve into laughter.

Depending upon how things are moving, time-wise, I sometimes ask at this point for a few people to stand and briefly share their high point story. I ask for stories that particularly well illustrate one or more of the emerging beliefs. When this works, it introduces some very moving testimony about the impact of the organization (or community) on someone's life and helps build the energy bonfire. When this doesn't work, it hands over control of the microphone to people who like and need attention. They may go on and on. So if you open the door, be prepared to graciously close it. It may mean approaching the speaker and standing beside him or her, looking expectantly for the mike. It may mean thanking the person as he or she is taking a breath and quickly bringing that segment to a close.

Having summarized our work to date, I send people on a well-deserved break (they've been working now for about 80 minutes), promising the main event upon their return.

SHARE YOUR DREAMS

After the break, I explain the next task, to share dreams, hopes, and aspirations for what the organization can achieve. Again, for a large group, it's useful to have a worksheet that summarizes these task instructions. See Appendix 10 for a sample.

As before, you can break a larger task into two halves to keep each part clear, simple, and manageable. First, ask people to work in pairs, sharing with a partner two or three dreams, hopes, and aspirations for the organization (or community) over the next two or three years. Remind people that they should focus on what they really want, not on how they get it. Ask people to record their contributions directly onto adhesive notes. We give these pairs only five or ten minutes for this task, so they must snap to it.

After time is up, we explain the final task for the small group. The groups have 25 minutes to accomplish three steps:

- Read aloud and post all ideas.
- Cluster ideas that are similar and give titles to groups of ideas.
- Choose the two or three best.

I briefly demonstrate how people will post, sort, and label their adhesive notes. Each group works at its table using a small flip chart. I remind people that they will be selecting two or three main goals that represent the best thinking at their table.

They may choose to pick a new group of leaders at this point, which further shares responsibility for success among all at the table. Or they may continue on with the same volunteers in the same roles. It is their choice.

Working as a table work group, people do a mini-version of what we will later do as a whole group: post, sort, label, and prioritize. If there are eight people at the table, sharing two to three hopes each, they must post and sort as many as 24 ideas. This requires a convenient flat work surface large enough to do this easily. A chart pad on an easel usually suffices. A wall can be helpful.

The *facilitator* asks a group member to read his or her three ideas aloud and post them on the group's flip chart. Then the second person reads and posts his or her ideas. New ideas should be posted apart from other ideas. Similar ideas should be clustered together. Each individual chooses where to post his or her ideas. Continue until everyone's ideas are posted and all similar ideas are posted together. The *recorder* helps people to post and sort.

Cluster Ideas and Name Them

Next, the *facilitator* briefly reviews each idea in a cluster of ideas and helps the group pick one idea that best captures the essence of all the notes in that grouping. Ask: *"Which note best captures the essence of this group of notes?"* Make that the title of the cluster. The *recorder* helps to post the titles on top of their groupings.

Then, the *facilitator* asks the group to choose two or three main goals, end results, or desired outcomes that represent the best thinking of the table. Ask: *"Of all these good ideas, which two or three represent our best thinking?"* Remember, groups should focus on what they want to see happen, not how difficult that might be to accomplish.

To be visible to all the participants in a large room, these goals must be written on something larger than 3' × 5' adhesive notes. You should supply each table with special supplies for the large group sharing. This could be a roll of 3" wide adding machine paper and scissors. Or it could be the top half of a page from a table top pad of self-adhesive flip chart pages. The *recorder* writes the goals for sharing with the larger group and then posts the strips or mini-posters.

See the Big Picture on a Vision Wall

You should have a Vision Wall ready to receive the contributions of each table. I love to have space enough for two long strips of brown kraft paper, one atop the other, each 4 feet wide and extending as far as 24 feet. That gives all of us plenty of room. Alternately, in a room full of doors, art work, light fixtures, and wood trim, we will import 4' × 8' sheets of foam core, 3/16" thick, to create a light, rigid internal wall.

I explain the posting and sorting process and ask for volunteers to start us off. Table representatives come to the front, one at a time, to read off their best visions of the future and post (with adhesive tape if needed) where appropriate. I help people find the right place, again grouping similar ideas.

Often, I find that *reporters* are able to read their contributions just fine, but are not able to help much with the posting. When people get close to the Vision Wall, they lose perspective on what is posted and can't quickly find similar items. So to keep things moving quickly, I help them out, suggesting a location or taking the mini-poster and posting it myself. This helps give some further shape and organization to the emerging themes, easing the sorting process that follows.

After the last group has posted its ideas, we read through all the ideas out loud once again, sorting them to be sure they are in the very best places. As with the small group process, any disagreement about an idea's ultimate location is resolved quickly by asking its authors to make the final call.

Next we capture the essence of the clustered ideas with a brightly colored title suggested by someone in the group. Here there is no author to turn to as final authority, so you should try to capture the sense of the group as best as you can. When you are done, the individual contributions of everyone in the room, distilled into the top recommendations of every table, are woven together into a common set of themes. This process takes just over half an hour with contributions from 8 to 10 tables.

If you have enough time, it is great to ask the group,

"What comments or reflections do you have on what you are seeing and hearing as a set of emerging themes?"

SELECT THE BEST

At this point the group's vision is clear yet expansive. We can now begin to think about turning the corner toward implementation. As in the small group process, I ask the group whether all the elements of the vision can be pursued simultaneously. If the answer is yes, we can celebrate right away and talk about next steps.

Most often the answer is no. There are too many good aspirations to complete them all with the time and resources that are available to the team, organization, or community. So some further distillation is required. Some have to happen before others. Some are more important than others. Some are just more appealing.

As in the small group process detailed in Chapter 6, we turn to multi-voting as a means for every individual in the room to express his or her preferences simultaneously in a way that gives an instant reading and record of the preferences of the whole group. I introduce it in much the same way, typically giving participants one dot for every three elements. Sometimes we just give participants three dots in all.

I review the major headers once again, draw clear targets on the brown paper to isolate each competing cluster, and ask people to make their choices in their seats. I will ask for a show of "thumbs up" to indicate when individuals have made their choices. When everyone is ready, I invite them to come up and place their dots.

Quickly, often with the help of volunteers, we tally the results and present them to the group. Once again, if you have enough time, it is great to ask everyone,

"What comments or reflections do you have on what you are seeing and hearing about your emerging priorities?"

PLAN NEXT STEPS

Planning next steps is even more important in the large group version of Grounded Visioning. Often there are people in the room that are not regular members of your organization or team. They may not be involved in ongoing implementation in a daily way. They want to know what will happen next with the important contributions that they have just made and with the good work that has just been completed. They want to know when they can expect what level of results as an outcome. They want to know who will be in touch with them, when, about progress updates.

This is also the time when enthusiasm among participants is often at its peak. If you are looking for volunteers, it is best, as the blacksmiths say, to "strike while the iron is hot." You have an open window of opportunity to enroll people into implementing the future that they have just created, and it may not last forever. In the case of the Clean Energy Council in Chapter 11, for example, the organizers quickly mapped out the governance challenge and the budget needs at the end of the meeting and participants spontaneously stood and pledged tens of thousands of dollars for the support of the Council.

You can finish your meeting in about four hours and still have about 25 minutes to map out clear next steps. Typically, this is a time for the meeting sponsor, representing his or her positional power and authority, to step forward. The sponsor spells out the composition of any groups that will be formed to detail the priorities that have emerged in the Grounded Vision. Appendix 12 shows one way to organize follow-up work, but there are many possibilities:

- You can organize by time, setting goals for each quarter, one year, and five years.
- You can organize by action steps.
- You can organize by goal, identifying steps and budget issues for each.

The sponsor typically makes promises about what will happen next, and by when. Participants are asked to volunteer for tasks if they are so inspired. People are so excited by this point that volunteer rates of 50 to 75 percent are not unusual. Appendix 13 features a sample volunteer sign-up form.

We sometimes ask participants to give the sponsors some feedback by completing a decidedly appreciative evaluation form, which asks questions like the following:

- What were the most significant outcomes of this day for you?
- On a scale of 1 to 10, how confident are you that we will achieve the results we defined today, and why?

Appendix 14 features a sample evaluation form.

AN ENERGETIC ENDING

Now that we have finished our work, we end in a way that is consistent with the positive spirit of the entire session. If I have had a chance to invite folks to share reasons for optimism along the way, I ask them to call them out now. In the relatively more complicated large group design, this question is typically omitted to save time. Given more time for the interview pairs, you can easily add this question and have people shout out their responses at this point.

More commonly I invite people to stand and share anything they appreciate about what has transpired: the group, the process, the results, someone's contribution, the food, anything at all. We take only a very few minutes to do this. Even so, participants invariably stand and share comments rich with heart and meaning. Usually, I give the sponsor the last word—typically a hearty thanks to everyone for their participation and contributions.

NOTES

1. Norman Vincent Peale, *Positive Thinking Every Day* (New York: Fireside, 1993).

2. Marvin R. Weisbord and Sandra Janoff, *Future Search: An Action Guide to Finding Common Ground in Organizations & Communities* (San Francisco: Berrett-Koehler, 1995), 180.

3. Ibid., 181.

Case Studies: Grounded Visioning for Large Groups

For some activities, the group subdivides and works in parallel.

There is nothing like a dream to create the future. Utopia today, flesh and blood tomorrow.

—Victor Hugo[1]

Sometimes, it is obvious that you have too many stakeholders to even consider the small group process. Then, as described in Chapter 8, you all need to work together in parallel to create your organization's Grounded Vision.

This chapter presents two case studies that demonstrate Grounded Visioning for large groups:

- A regional horticultural society that brought together 70 people to begin the process of reversing its decline.
- A loose amalgam of leaders in a state's nonprofit sector that organized a Grounded Visioning session for 250 participants.

As you read these cases and think about your own large group application, ask yourself these questions:

- Who are the people who feel a stake in the future of your team, company, organization, or community and would want to be in the room discussing it?
- What is at stake in the evolution of your team, company, organization, or community that would bring these people to a meeting and have them freely give their time and talent?

Grounded Visioning Gets Results

Organization: Horticultural Society
Planning need: Turnaround organization in decline
Result: Supporters dare to invest again in a renewed vision

Organization: Statewide Nonprofit Association
Planning need: Unify nonprofit sector by defining a common agenda
Result: New statewide nonprofit organization with 400 members and increased clout

---

- If size and space were not a limiting factor, how many people would you want to participate in creating that future?
- What fears or concerns about convening such a large group would you have to overcome in order to gain the value from their attendance and participation?

HORTICULTURAL SOCIETY FACES UP TO FINANCIAL DECLINE AND MEMBER DESERTION

A statewide Horticultural Society was, in its executive director's words, a "tired organization." Its long history of proud achievements failed to protect it from first a slow—and eventually a swift—disintegration into a quagmire of controversy, error, financial trouble, and member abandonment. The new executive director was hired to lead a turnaround, and he turned to Grounded Visioning for help. He brought together every significant stakeholder, about 70 people, for four hours.

The executive director tells the story best in his own words:

The steam had almost run out for the 178-year-old horticultural society. All of the education programs were halted, except one, and the membership was at record low levels. The cornerstone event for the society—the Spring Flower Show—had lost attendance every year for a decade. The Society's historic headquarters had been sold, precious rare books were damaged in a flood, and the finances were hanging on by a thread. Board members had been running the organization for almost two years after the previous director had resigned in disgrace. Everyone associated with the society seemed discouraged and disgruntled.

This is when we were invited to help. When the Society hired the new executive director, he immediately sought consultant assistance to facilitate a process to begin envisioning a new future for this tired old organization.

Preparation Makes Large Groups Productive

The Grounded Visioning session brought together more than 70 people interested in the society's future. Participants included trustees, overseers, key donors,

Table 9.1
Horticultural Society
A Half-Day Grounded Visioning Agenda

Time (minutes)	Task
15	Welcome
65	• Explain task
	• Share high point stories at table work groups
	• List common themes in table work groups
	• Report themes to the large group
15	Break
90	• Explain task
	• Share dreams, hopes, and aspirations in pairs
	• List common goals in table work groups
	• Report, post, and sort goals into themes
25	Plan next steps

master garden volunteers, senior staff, members of sister agencies, business people in the green industry, neighbors, society members, and members of garden society partners.

These were the ambitious goals for the four-hour Grounded Visioning session:

- Share what is best about the Society in a fun and positive way.
- Set key goals for the Society's desired achievements for the next two or three years.
- Set up goal teams for action planning as part of a strategic plan.

Before the meeting, participants received packets containing a brief history of the society, a meeting agenda, a list of invited participants, a summary of the society's mission and values, trend data about budget and membership, and a personal update from the executive director. Receiving this information before the meeting gave participants a chance to reflect in advance on the challenges facing the organization and the mission and values that had served it well for many years.

Everyone was invited to come an hour early for an optional brown bag lunch and tour of the gardens. Then, people found their assigned seats at round tables set for 8 to 10, arranged to ensure maximum diversity in every table work group conversation.

Table 9.1 shows the agenda for the Grounded Visioning session.

Personal Memories Set Optimistic Tone

The introductory welcome featured a request that each of the various stakeholder groups—trustees, overseers, staff, volunteers, donors, etc.—stand when their group name was called, to give everyone a quick visual perspective as to the extraordinary diversity that was present in the room.

Because this was such a large group, the appreciative interviews were streamlined to just two questions:

- What has been a high point in your experience of the Society? Participants went around the circle to share their responses at their tables.
- What are your two or three dreams, hopes, and aspirations for the next two or three years?

"Beginning by working in small groups to identify special and personal memories associated with the Society, the tone of the day laid a positive outlook as the foundation for the remainder of the day's discussions," said the society's executive director.

Based on these memories, each table identified common themes, which were then shared with the large group as a finish to the open-ended sentence, "When our Society is at its best, we..."

- Are inspired to be at our best, and we inspire others by demonstrating excellence.
- Are inspired to work to achieve our goals, and follow through on a clear set of priorities.
- Are inclusive and receptive to all.
- Are excited to learn more and educate others.
- Attract a large audience to our beautiful gardens at the Flower Show.
- Connect plants and people.
- Offer a place of peace and beauty, such as our gardens in bloom.
- Preserve the best of the past (our horticultural knowledge) and lead into the future.
- Generate enthusiasm in horticulture and a love for the environment and healthy gardening.
- Provide people with the resources and inspiration to work together in the pursuit of horticulture.
- Provide value to our membership in education, entertainment, volunteerism, and success in horticulture.

This approach of letting the whole group identify common themes respected all the people in the room, many of whom held strong beliefs and were quite distressed by the society's decline.

Seventy People Share Dreams for the Future

Answers to the second question—what are your two or three dreams, hopes, and aspirations for the next two or three years—were shared first in pairs and then with their tablemates. Then, as a table group, participants chose the top two or three goals that represented the best thinking at the table.

This structure meant that, even with 70 people, everyone was heard. The executive director commented:

No one person dominated the discussion and everyone had the opportunity to contribute to the final list of priorities. The final product was a very concrete set of priorities for the organization. This was interpreted into a year-long strategy for improvement, widely supported by the organization's key stakeholders.

Nearly 40 distinct aspirations emerged in from the many contributions brought forward, and these were further clustered into six high-level aspirations:

- **Attain financial strength.** Create strategic fund development plan, build relationships with donors, increase membership (12,000–14,000 members), increase volunteerism and donations through reconnection with garden clubs, strengthen trustee contribution, increase garden home visitation and revenues, strengthen flower show (125,000–150,000 attendance), obtain corporate sponsorships, conduct capital campaign, and build endowment.
- **Develop garden home as world class.** Create site master plan with engaging vision, be a year-round destination, create new gardens at Elm Bank, create education center of excellence at Elm Bank, find donor for Japanese garden, restore manor house, initiate summer flower show, and boost staffing and volunteerism at garden.
- **Provide educational outreach.** Serve diverse and underserved communities, expand people capacity for outreach, expand educational programming, and build on collection.
- **Do an aggressive marketing campaign.** Develop strategic marketing and public relations plan, boost visibility through partnerships, reach out to key constituents in targeted way, boost volunteerism, increase media presence, create summer flower show, enhance web site, boost visual identity, build stronger internal capacity to market effectively, and better communicate what we do.
- **Develop the downtown garden.** Organize to take action, promote interim use, realize long-term vision, and increase advocacy for public green spaces.
- **Achieve operational excellence.** Develop strategic plan, improve work processes, and integrate environmental ethic into everything we do.

Inclusive Planning Grows Enthusiasm

According to the executive director, "The many participants emerged from the day energized and more hopeful." As the afternoon drew to a close, participants were asked to volunteer to help implement the strategies they had mapped out in their work groups. More than half the participants volunteered, including three who were willing to lead their teams.

The work groups met throughout the summer to further understand the society's current situation, identify possible strategies for action, and set priorities. Their priorities formed the basis of a strategic vision document that guided the decision-making of the executive director during his tenure.

The executive director reflected,

The last few years of enormous effort have resulted in a much stronger institution. That Grounded Visioning session has been extremely valuable and appreciated in turning around such a troubled place. The recent Flower Show was a great success programmatically and financially. The Society now has more financial resources than in many, many years. The education programs are thriving and our garden home is approaching public garden levels of maintenance and plantings. The new gift shop was a huge financial success at the Flower Show and at our garden home, far exceeding financial projections. The downtown garden project is secure with a new agreement in place to collaborate. Membership has grown from 4,100 when I was hired to close to 7,000! Longtime donors and members of the philanthropic community, some of whom attended the Grounded Visioning session, began to increase their financial support and to get re-involved with the organization.

STATEWIDE NONPROFIT ASSOCIATION: CAN 25,000 ORGANIZATIONS COLLABORATE?

This case is an extreme example of scaling Grounded Visioning to work with large groups.

A group of nonprofit leaders, numbering as many as 65, began meeting monthly in the largest city in the state. They called themselves the Working Group. Membership was open to anyone who shared their passion. Their focus: repositioning the state's nonprofit sector to attain greater clout, to garner more deserved public recognition, and to strengthen the sector.

A program officer of a leading foundation supporting the effort reflected on the drivers pushing these busy leaders together at the time:

> The effort started with the post 9/11 recession and the burst of the technology bubble, when the economy was a disaster. Private donations were down, public funding shifted to security, and there were massive cutbacks to the nonprofit sector. The blame game started, and senior people in state government started questioning the competence of those in the sector, which was totally unfair. Something had to be done to improve the image of the sector and increase its clout.

In nearly 40 states around the country, leaders like these had formed statewide nonprofit associations to promote these agendas. This state was home to 25,000 nonprofits, representing 21,345 public charities and 4,191 private foundations, in a vibrant nonprofit sector. But the sector had no statewide association and therefore no collective voice.

Years before, the various subsets of the nonprofit sector—human services, community development, arts, education, health care—in the state had formed their own individual statewide trade associations. Many nonprofits had been organized, but not in ways that promoted the health of the sector as a whole. The sector had no way to organize itself around the issues that were important to everyone. And many smaller nonprofits lacked any affiliations and seemed to possess no collective voice whatsoever. The Working Group hoped to craft a strategy to enable the nonprofit sector to speak effectively with one voice.

Jumble of Nonprofit Associations Can't Find Its Voice

But there were obstacles. People tended to identify with their existing groups. They would work hard to benefit their own but not necessarily extend themselves for the common good. Nonprofit leaders had tried to find their collective voice in the past. Good people would come together, work hard, make false starts, and end with little to show for their efforts. The veterans—many of them members of the Working Group—could recount a list of half a dozen failed starts over the past decade.

Nevertheless, the need was overwhelming. Nonprofit workers accounted for a quarter of the state's workforce and pumped $50 billion into the state's economy through jobs and the purchase of goods and services. Nonprofits raised billions in private donations to supplement and enhance essential services, improve the quality of life, and enrich communities with art and music. Nonprofit agencies managed $2.5 billion in state contracts, serving the state's most needy residents.

Yet the sector could not find its voice. The Working Group labored on, like a rock climber who can't climb up and can't climb down, committed, but stuck in a perilous position. This is where Grounded Visioning came in.

How to Organize a Statewide Meeting?

The Working Group decided to convene a statewide Nonprofit Summit that would aim to create a common agenda and a mechanism to implement it. The Working Group imagined a large group of executive directors, nonprofit leaders, policymakers, stakeholders, consultants, academics, donors, and individuals with a passion and commitment to build a powerful nonprofit sector. They invited me to design and facilitate the summit.

A big event like this casts a big shadow. We laid out a calendar on a large wall at one Working Group meeting and began brainstorming the outcomes that would make the Nonprofit Summit a success. Each outcome suggested a series of time-consuming organizing tasks:

- If the summit was to be inclusive, it had to be large enough to accommodate anyone with the passion to come. That meant lots of outreach.
- If the summit was to be recognized as legitimate, it had to be not just large, but diverse, across many dimensions. That meant lots of targeted outreach.
- If the summit was to be effective in building a common agenda, it needed to build its vision organically from the insights of many people across the state. That meant lots of regional outreach.
- If the summit was to be effective in building a mechanism to implement the common agenda, it had to feature hardheaded research on the best thinking the sector had to offer. That meant lots of homework.

The list kept getting longer, and the summit date kept getting pushed back further and further.

Eleven Regional Meetings Set the Stage

We realized from these conversations that we needed to hold a series of regional meetings throughout the state in advance of the summit, engaging non-profit stakeholders in the conversation about the sector, educating them about the potential power of the sector, promoting the idea of the summit, and seeking their views as to what a shared common agenda might include. The networking and organizing to convene these regional meetings would lay the groundwork for the eventual success of the summit. So the Working Group took what appeared to be a major detour on its path to the summit and set about organizing 11 regional meetings instead.

The 11 two-hour meetings were a great success. More than 500 nonprofit representatives attended, and each heard a brief presentation about the Working Group, the nonprofit sector, and the challenge. Most of each meeting was given to conversation about three key questions:

- What problems are you facing locally?
- What is a potential common agenda for the sector?
- If there were a statewide mechanism to advocate for nonprofits and tell their story effectively, what would it look like and how would you get there?

Ninety-eight percent of the participants endorsed the idea of organizing non-profits in a formal way. Slowly but surely the information and the interest trickled up. A statewide meeting of nonprofit advocates began at long last to seem inevitable, and the notion of finding common ground grew more plausible. The grassroots path to success appeared open.

The final meetings were not regional meetings, per se, but rather meetings of the leadership of the state's many nonprofit trade associations. With some trepidation, the Working Group invited all of these powerful leaders to come together in one room and hear its plans. Each of them could easily consider a new state-wide association to be a competitor. After a polite hearing, each began to speak. One by one, each expressed the view that this new association would not compete with them for their current network members, but would instead tie them into the strength of a greater network. Some offered to serve on the founding board. The players who could have killed it instead blessed it. The political path to success now appeared open at last!

Can 250 People Meet Productively?

A handsome four-page invitation to the Nonprofit Summit, designed as an electronic PDF file, was e-mailed to the hundreds of people who had attended regional meetings or expressed interest. The promised outcomes were a common nonprofit action agenda and a mechanism for carrying it out. The summit was free (subsidized by leadership foundations) and spanned two days. The first day would be devoted to visioning and the formation of the common agenda. The second day would be devoted to the means to carry out that agenda.

The heart of the first day was a Grounded Visioning exercise, adapted for the unique constraints of the situation. At the Grounded Visioning session, there would be 250 nonprofit representatives in their seats, ready to work. The core

Table 9.2
Agenda for the Nonprofit Summit

Time (minutes)	Task
15	Opening
70	High points and beliefs
15	Break
110	Common agenda
60	Lunch
105	Desired results
15	Break
45	Reports
15	Closing

Grounded Visioning activity started the summit and was completed by lunch. Table 9.2 shows the agenda.

Success Stories Build Connection, Enthusiasm

For Grounded Visioning sessions of any size, appreciative interviews play a pivotal role in building community very quickly. In this situation, the 250 participants were organized in 31 tables of eight, assigned so as to be seated with people they did not know. People shared their high point stories at the tables to serve multiple purposes: to allow new tablemates to introduce themselves, to build community, and to share some essence about the nonprofit sector. In this case the appreciative question was:

"Share a story of a high point in your experience of the state's nonprofit sector, when you felt most committed, engaged, proud, and inspired."

Each person had two minutes each to share, and then tables were instructed to find the common themes in all the stories they had just heard. Next, based on these stories, tables identified one or two beliefs, completing the sentence, "When we in nonprofit organizations are at our best, we..." The activity came to a rousing finish when reporters from each table shared their conclusions in 31 quick 30-second reports.

What flowed effortlessly to the surface was an incisive view of the heart of the sector, with reporters sharing that, at their best, people in the sector:

- Work to contribute to the improvement of the quality of life of the entire community.
- Empower people to accomplish goals they otherwise couldn't, and thereby grow.
- Believe that we have the power to make change in people's lives and in society.
- Serve as a catalyst for making a difference by creating opportunities for a richer life.
- Take actions that produce stronger communities.
- Believe in the value of human beings and their ability to effect change in their lives toward a vision of a world that is more just.

Each brief statement of belief, distilled from a short list of common themes from a small sample of stories, was like a log tossed on an energetic bonfire that began burning bright in the room, captivating everyone with its collective power and light.

Fresh Ideas Combined with the Best from the Planning Meeting

The participants returned after a break ready to attend to the vision of a Common Agenda. Suggestions from the regional meetings formed the basis for a starting vision. The many themes that had been voiced and recorded in those 11 meetings had been distilled down to a set of 10 potential themes:

- Creating capacity to access greater resources.
- Promoting operational savings from collaboration.
- Sharing best practices widely.
- Increasing nonprofit sector employee benefits.
- Finding, attracting, and retaining talent for the sector.
- Increasing public awareness and valuing of the sector.
- Increasing public valuing of the sector's clients.
- Gathering research data on the sector's impact on society.
- Changing public policy by increasing advocacy.
- Increasing government support (from taxes) while decreasing government burden (from regulation).

Each of the 10 themes, along with about a dozen supporting points that had given rise to each theme, formed the set of potential items in the common agenda. These were documented in handouts and with posters on a Vision Wall surrounding the participants.

Participants were asked first in pairs, and then in tables, to confer as to whether any additional candidates for the common agenda should be brought forward. The organizers had done their best to synthesize what had been heard at the regional meetings, but this step ensured that nothing essential was missed.

These additional ideas were heard and posted along with the starting list.

Multi-Voting Means All 250 Participants Have a Say

When all additional ideas had been heard and posted, the participants were invited to express their preferences, through multi-voting. Three clear priorities emerged:

Figure 9.1
Multi-voting makes preferences obvious: Everyone votes simultaneously, so every vote has equal weight.

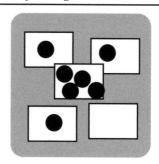

Illustration by Cindy Murphy.

- Advocacy
- Public awareness
- Organizational effectiveness

The final task of the visioning segment of the Nonprofit Summit was for table work groups to take one of these three topics and identify short-term and long-term results that would indicate successful fulfillment in their area. The large body reorganized itself into three groups by interest area and, supported by facilitators brought in just for this task, set to work in parallel.

An additional round of posting and sorting of their ideas and setting priorities quickly by multi-voting led to three sets of highly desired outcomes framed in results language. The final work product listed the three main goals, with three long-term and three short-term results specified for each. It formed the organizing basis of the state's first-ever statewide nonprofit association. The Common Agenda animated an emerging organization that built a respected board, attracted a talented executive director and staff, and gained a membership of 400 nonprofits in its first year.

Two years later, the program officer whose foundation was a lead supporter reflected on the summit's impact. "Now we have an entity that speaks on behalf of the sector. There is someone to call, and someone to give voice to the sector's concerns. We have created a group purchasing program, and a common training database, and a pro bono legal service. We have helped pass critical legislation improving the lives of workers in the sector."

In looking ahead, she commented, "Once again our economy is going into a tailspin, and we need this association more than ever. Times are getting tight again, and the work we started is not done. It is so important for the sector to be more together. And interestingly, the people we were most concerned about— the subsector trade associations—are the ones who are now most involved and engaged in policy work and board work. They know we need a strong collective voice—for strong programs, and strong organizations."

NOTE

1. Victor Hugo, *Les Misérables* (1862).

—————— 10 ——————

Vision into Action

Even before you create the vision, create the template to follow through.

Vision without action is a daydream. Action without vision is a nightmare.

—Japanese proverb

The end of a Grounded Visioning session is a time of excitement and hope. Participants have dug deep to discover the best in themselves. They have shared private dreams and discovered common aspirations with their peers. They can now imagine a positive future, and they like it! This is the time to engage them in making initial commitments to make it real.

With its focus on speed, Grounded Visioning is more of an event than a process. The many people who have little patience with process will find this refreshing. But follow-through is still vital and necessary.

A Grounded Visioning session itself does not create the future. A Grounded Visioning session creates a greater possibility of the envisioned future and opens the door to realizing it.

LEAVE THE GROUNDED VISIONING SESSION WITH AN IMPLEMENTATION PLAN

Therefore, as the session ends you should put into practice strategies for translating vision into action. You need to plan out these implementation strategies *before* the Grounded Visioning session.

At first, this seems counterintuitive. After all, the vision is going to come out of the meeting. How is it possible to plan implementation strategies before you know what the vision will be?

In actuality, though, it is possible to apply a standard planning template to just about any goal:

- State the goal.
- Define indicators and measures of success.
- Define strategies to achieve the goal and meet those indicators.
- Define major milestones of achievement linked to the indicators.
- Define action steps to implement those strategies and achieve those milestones.
- Define persons responsible and time frames.

You can ask people to do this during the Grounded Visioning session itself, right after a break. Or you can ask people to sort themselves into groups by interest and meet later.

WHAT HAPPENS NEXT?

Most organizations choose to follow up by formulating action teams of one type or another. This gives small groups of individuals—presumably those with the greatest interest and/or skill—the chance to take the great ideas developed in the very quick visioning session and develop them into more detailed action plans.

Before the Grounded Visioning session, you or your planning team should decide how you want to follow up:

- Are the Grounded Visioning results recommendations or decisions?
- Will you form implementation teams immediately or allow some time for ideas to settle?
- Do you want volunteers, or will you assign people to teams?
- Will teams choose leaders, or will you appoint leaders?
- Will you define the team's task, or will the team define the task?
- Should teams decide on action steps, or should you give them a planning template?
- Are these planning meetings separate or integrated with other activities?

Make the Trade-off between Enthusiasm and Control

Are the Grounded Visioning results recommendations or decisions? This is an important choice. You can use the goals that have emerged from the visioning process as they are, or you can empower your planning committee to review and revise them. In the first instance, the large group is making decisions, albeit quick ones; in the second, it is making recommendations to another body. Either way each chartered goal team needs a clear, target goal. I have seen either approach work. It pays to tell the large group in advance, though, whether its work is creating a set of recommendations for others or a set of decisions. Going with the group members' recommendations, wherever they lead you, ensures you capture their full support. Going with your synthesis of the group's recommendations ensures you can live with what you must implement.

Will you form implementation teams immediately or allow some time for ideas to settle? You can form goal teams on the spot and set them to work immediately, or you can start them up after a period of reflection. Either way you need to give them time and space to meet and work together. Either way works. Forming teams on the spot allows the energy of the visioning process to infuse the implementation planning process right away. Forming teams after a period of reflection ensures a more measured approach to the task at hand.

Find the Right Mix of Self-Determination and Guidance

Do you want volunteers, or will you assign people to teams? You can ask for volunteers who wish to work on goal teams, or you can assign individuals to goal teams. Either way the teams need motivated members. I strongly recommend that you ask for volunteers. That way you are more likely to have people who both care and are willing to take responsibility for getting results. The downside of asking for volunteers is that sometimes the people with the needed skills or leadership ability fail to volunteer. And people who bring serious interpersonal shortcomings or strident personal agendas may volunteer. So, starting with a list of committed volunteers, you have the option of subtracting people who just won't work (if you wish) and adding people who will contribute skills, perspective, and balance (if you must).

Figure 10.1

Ask for volunteers: Committed volunteers take responsibility for results.

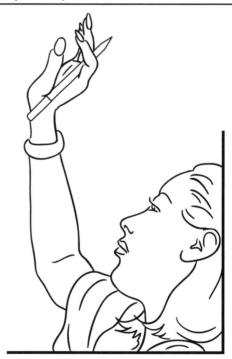

Illustration by Cindy Murphy.

Will teams choose leaders, or will you appoint leaders? You can ask goal teams to select their own leadership, or you can assign leadership. Either way the teams need leadership. We can go either way with this choice. Allowing a team to choose its own leadership invests that person with the authority of the team. But the team may not always pick the best leader or the one who will work best with the leaders of other teams. Should you assign leadership, presumably you'll select the best person for the job, thus ensuring that the job will be done to your specifications. But that person will have to earn the respect of his or her team.

Help Teams Work Consistently

Will you define the team's task, or will the team define the task? You can ask your goal teams to define their own charge as best as they can, or you can define a charge for them. Either way the teams need a clear charge. We strongly recommend that you map out a charge for each team. To help you we have identified the kinds of questions we feel must be answered in advance in "Give Teams Structure So They Succeed." Goal teams can always push back to their sponsors for clarifications, or changes, in their charge.

Should teams decide on action steps, or should you give them a planning template? You can ask teams to use their best judgment in completing the task, or you can give them an action planning template which, once completed, means they've done the job to your specifications. I strongly recommend you design and use an action planning template to guide the work of all groups in a uniform direction. That way you won't end up with apples and oranges when all the teams have completed their work. You can see a sample action planning template in Appendix 12.

Are these planning meetings separate or integrated with other activities? You can think of the goal teams as performing an independent planning exercise, or you can see them integrating their work into your existing planning, operations, and budgeting cycles. I strongly recommend that you think of the work of the goal teams as feeding into your existing planning, operations, and budgeting cycles. I suggest that you continue to modify your goal teams' charge, composition strategy, and action planning template until you are sure that the results of the Grounded Visioning session, as advanced by the goal teams, will feed directly into those existing planning cycles. This is the single best way to increase the probability that your visionary thinking actually gets implemented.

FOCUS ON THE FUTURE

Grounded Visioning creates a vision of the future but it doesn't tell you explicitly how to get there. Grounded Visioning generates enthusiasm among participants to create that future, but it doesn't tell you how to channel that enthusiasm. It is an axiom of the organizational development field that "people support what they help create," so by engaging people in creating their future, you can count on their support in making it happen.

There are many great tools and templates to help teams implement goals successfully. You will find excellent resources in the two fantastic books on teams featured in the resource box in this chapter. The trick is to find the means that fit with the culture of your team, company, organization, or community and then support them fully in being successful.

Give Teams Structure So They Succeed

Sample Questions for Goal Teams

Overall Purpose

- What is the team's assignment?

Results Expected

- What will a successful outcome look like?

Completion Date

- When must the team's work be completed?

Resources Provided

- What financial, technical, and administrative assistance does the team have?

Constraints

- What parameters bound the work of the team?

Team Sponsor

- Who will sponsor the team?

Team Members

- Who will serve on the team?
- With what skills?
- Who will lead the team?

Approval Points

- At what points does the team need approval before proceeding to its next step?

Time Commitment

- What is the expected time commitment for members?

Special Instructions

- What specific guidance is offered to ensure the team's success?

> **Learn More from These Great Books on Teams**
>
> *Simple yet Powerful Tools to Support Team Improvement Projects*
>
> *The Team Handbook,* 3rd ed. by Barbara J. Streibel, Brian L. Joiner, and Peter Scholtes (Madison, WI: Joiner/Oriel Inc., 2003).
>
> *Highly Visual Tools to Support the Fast, Strong Start-ups of Teams*
>
> *Team Startup: Creating Gameplans for Success* (The Grove Consultants International, 2008).
> www.grove.com.

My experience of visioning with teams is that the expression of people's great ideas builds up a reservoir of energy that is like water behind a dam—it wants to be released! Finding the right implementation vehicle—typically through teams but perhaps through other means—creates a channel for the expression of this great reservoir of people energy. People naturally want to create. They naturally want to follow through on their passions. What they so often lack in organizations is clarity about their direction, a vehicle for expressing their passion for that direction, and support for their initiative to move in that direction. When they have that clarity, that vehicle, and that support, the implementation of the Grounded Vision can be as easy, fast, and fun as creating it.

11

Case Studies: Vision into Action

The more specific the metrics and plan, the more successful the innovation.

Enough words have been exchanged; now at last let me see some deeds!
—Johann Wolfgang von Goethe, *Faust I*

G rounded Visioning, for most organizations, is an event. It stands apart from your daily activities as a work team, volunteer organization, or community. For that reason, it's important for the sponsoring organization to follow through on the insights and revelations of common ground that typically emerge in a Grounded Visioning session to merge it with the ongoing life of the organization.

This chapter shows how two organizations followed through, or failed to follow through, on the results of their Grounded Visioning sessions:

- Trade association of clean energy businesses: Buy-in at the highest levels of government encouraged a flourishing group of task forces that pursued ambitious, measurable targets by achieving clear milestones along the way.
- Natural foods company: Lack of commitment at the ownership level meant that the Grounded Visioning was a one-day, feel-good event, and not the beginning of a process for creating a new future.

In the first case, slow but steady efforts harvested much of the value that emerged from the brief but powerful visioning session. While the clean energy trade association did not realize all its dreams quickly, it did break new ground, and built a foundation for substantial gains in the near future. It returned again and again along its path to the participative style of the Grounded Visioning session. In fact, that inclusive planning style became a distinctive competency and a cherished value in the success of the collaborative enterprise.

Grounded Visioning Gets Results

Organization: Clean Energy Council
Planning need: Cohesive voice for diverse industry
Result: Clear metrics and targets drive change

Organization: Natural Foods Company
Planning need: How to maintain values in wake of ownership and market changes
Result: Lack of management buy-in means no follow-through to Grounded Visioning

---

In the second case, the sale to venture capitalists of controlling interest in the company brought changes that essentially gutted the employees' original vision. The changes, while intended to leave the brand intact, resulted in the attrition of most of the people who created it and who might have kept the original vision alive. These actions are a humble reminder of how abruptly a vision can be undone.

These cases show some of the many factors that can affect the success of your implementation:

- Having real structure to follow-ups, with multiple committees.
- Making dreams measurable, with targets you can refer back to afterward.
- Getting buy-in from stakeholders, which pays off in the long run.
- Creating excitement for your meeting even before it starts with advance publicity.

As you read these cases, think about the powerful forces that may either support or hinder the success of the implementation of your Grounded Vision. Peter Block gave us a wonderful map[1] to the political landscape of organizations that often determines the success or failure of a venture (Table 11.1).

Block showed us that agreement and trust are the key dimensions in winning support from others for our vision. Those whom we trust and who agree with us on the merits of our vision are our allies. Those whom we don't trust and who don't agree with us on the merits of our vision are our adversaries. Those whom we trust and yet who disagree with us on the merits of our vision are our "respected opposition." Those whom we don't trust and yet who happen to

Table 11.1
Map of the Political Landscape of Organizations

	Low trust	High trust
High agreement	Strange bedfellows	Allies
Low agreement	Adversaries	Respected opposition

agree with us on the merits of our vision, for whatever reason, are our "strange bedfellows."

You could say that the clean energy council did a better job of mobilizing its allies and collaborating with its strange bedfellows and respected opposition than did the employees in the natural foods company.

Think about the likely elements of your Grounded Vision. Who are the allies whom you trust, and with whom you agree, that you can count on to support it? Who would be your adversaries? Strange bedfellows? Respected opposition? How best could you mobilize your supporters and neutralize the rest?

As you read these cases, think about how things actually get done in your organization. When you reflect on past successes, ask yourself what made them possible? What enabled a great new idea to become just "the way we do things around here"? How did an innovation get integrated into operations at your organization and become a new routine?

Many of these classic implementation strategies may have been integral to these past successes:

- Recruiting a passionate champion to make it happen.
- Charging an empowered, cross-functional team to make it happen.
- Employing project management discipline to make it happen.
- Influencing key opinion leaders to win their support to make it happen.
- Borrowing resources on a pilot basis to make it happen.

What strategies are key to successful follow-through in your organization?

CLEAN ENERGY COUNCIL: INDUSTRY SEEKS A UNITED VOICE

"Here's the thing," said the new governor's new energy secretary. He was speaking in March to a room full of executives from solar, wind power, fuel cell, and ethanol companies at a business presentation competition for clean energy enterprise. "This state needs a united force for the clean energy industry. Solar wants one thing. Wind wants another. There is no comprehensive voice on the policy side."

The energy secretary reminded the executives what the Biotechnology Council had done for the state in the 1980s in creating a vibrant biotechnology industry. He reminded them what the Telecommunications Council had done for the state in the 1990s in creating a vibrant telecommunications industry. He argued that now was the time for a new Clean Energy Council to do the same for the state's burgeoning clean energy economy. He expressed hope that a new trade association would give the industry a stronger voice, focus its lobbying power, and foster more creativity by connecting investors, entrepreneurs, academics, and policymakers.

"We want to help you. Make it easy for us," he concluded.

One executive stood up and said, "I want to work on that." Others approached him afterward and offered to help. A few people decided to form a planning group. Their aim: to involve all the clean energy stakeholder groups and tap their wisdom in a council led by industry.

Government Officials Struggle to Build Consensus in Diverse Industry

Everywhere they went people loved the idea. "There is a huge void, a gaping need, and the time is right," they would say. "But," they would always add, "you will be herding cats. These people—these CEOs—they don't work well together. If you get them in a room together it will be chaotic. They will not get along. These people do battle against each other every day in the marketplace."

The lead organizer later reflected, "That was the one, major hurdle we faced." This is when I was invited to help.

The charge was as clear as the obstacles. The planning committee wanted 100 green energy CEOs working together in a room for the first time. The committee thought it could coax maybe half a day from these bosses, but not a minute more. The committee wanted a big bang, in the form of three big outcomes:

- Create a common vision of the state clean energy economy.
- Identify acceleration initiatives for achieving this vision.
- Form a self-sustaining council of clean energy stakeholders to advance this agenda.

Table 11.2 shows the agenda for the four-hour meeting.

Advance Publicity Creates a Must-Attend Grounded Visioning Session

As it learned about Grounded Visioning, the planning committee began to think this might really work. "This is the solution," said the lead organizer:

I had an amazing sense of faith that it would work. We felt a huge amount of excitement and urgency about the council idea. We knew we needed a united policy voice right away. Yet we backed off on the idea of just announcing the Clean Energy Council. We decided we can't just tell folks what to do. Instead we decided to let

Table 11.2
Agenda: Clean Energy CEOs

Time (minutes)	Task
10	Opening
15	Overview of the state clean energy economy by high-level policymaker
75	Envisioning top five metrics and targets for 2020, setting priorities
15	Break
75	Envisioning top five acceleration initiatives in the next two to three years
50	Creating a Clean Energy Council, closing

the stakeholders speak, and hope they would agree. We put our council concept in our pocket. Because of how we were going about this, we knew that whatever came out would be the right answer. We had confidence in the process. We became excited, and curious about what would happen.

The Stakeholders' Roundtable was set for June. Meanwhile, the energy secretary was quoted in the paper as saying, "Here...you don't have a particularly visible public voice for clean energy firms. The governor is saying, 'I want this sector to be a big deal.'"[2] The governor invited two dozen green energy CEOs to meet with him in his office in a highly visible meeting. One of the two dozen CEOs spoke afterward with the papers about the Stakeholders' Roundtable, "The way things are going, it might be standing room only. I think the governor is very genuine in his interest"[3] in promoting the sector. The word was out, and the phone started ringing off the hook. Every CEO in the sector wanted to be in the room.

Energy CEOs Need Little Prompting to Identify Metrics and Targets

On the morning of the meeting, the large room overlooking the city skyline filled with men and women in suits. Participants took their designated seats at round tables of eight, assigned to ensure a maximum diversity of sector participation at every table. The sponsors made their welcome, the energy secretary gave his overview, and the stage was set. In fact, given the excitement in the room, and our very short time frame, we dispensed with the appreciative interviews and went right to visioning.

We challenged each table work group to answer two questions in 30 minutes:

- What are the top five metrics we should use to express our vision of a robust state clean energy economy in 2020?
- For each of these metrics, what targets do we want to reach by 2020?

We provided them with a list of roles by which to organize themselves to effectively manage the task, a worksheet with the task written out, and a handout with metrics used by other states to define their clean energy economies. The participants at the tables barely waited for the task to be explained before they rushed into work.

Soon reporters from tables were bringing forward their completed metrics, and associated targets, to post them on the Vision Wall. To save time, the metrics posters and their associated targets were posted and sorted as they were finished, so by the time half the room was done the other half could already see a set of emerging themes. After a quick review and sorting of the metrics, participants were given a chance to indicate their top five preferences, using adhesive dots. By two hours into the morning, the CEOs had defined five metrics and five associated targets for a robust state clean energy economy by 2020:

- Leadership (#1 state in research and development, start-ups, capital and company funding).
- Jobs (200,000 clean energy jobs).
- Efficiency (30 percent reduction in per capita energy use).
- Renewables (increasing use to 25–30 percent of energy sources).
- Greenhouse gas emissions (25–30 percent reduction).

Table Groups Work Efficiently to Identify Priorities

After a short break, on to the next challenge! The table work groups were tasked with two more questions to answer in another 30 minutes:

- What are the top acceleration initiatives we need to implement in the next two to three years to be on track to achieve our 2020 targets?
- What are the top five initiatives we most want to see implemented in the next two to three years?

Of the many acceleration initiatives proposed, by far the most popular was the need to "identify skill gaps and educate the future workforce." In fact, several months later, the group followed up with an entire half-day visioning session, with invited representatives from education, trade schools, unions, large end users, utilities, conservation groups, and community colleges. This second group conducted another Grounded Visioning session in direct response to this proposal.

Other initiatives included the following:

- Create an energy efficiency plan tied to economic growth.
- Put the state on the global clean energy map by building closer relationships between CEOs and national media.
- Bridge the entrepreneurs' "valley of death" (apologies to Alfred, Lord Tennyson) by creating supports to move new technologies from the lab to commercialization to private financing.
- Attract global energy R&D divisions to relocate to the region.

Groundwork for the Clean Energy Trade Association

Most of the final hour was set aside for organizing conversations about a new clean energy trade association. The members of the planning committee came to the front, walked people through the major choices before them, and made some smart recommendations. During these discussions, a number of CEOs stood and made pledges, totaling in the tens of thousands of dollars, for financing this new venture.

Two issues emerged to threaten the dramatic, emerging consensus:

- Was a regional, rather than a statewide, organization more appropriate, given the regional structure of the utility grid?

- Would this organization duplicate a recently formed peer support network of CEOs, convened by well funded venture capitalists, partly to help those VC firms enter the sector?

The concerns were noted, and the organizers asked for volunteers to help birth this new entity and tackle these questions. Then, they invited everyone to have lunch.

Many Subcommittees Follow Up on Clean Energy Targets

A newly formed advisory board, using volunteers from the Stakeholders' Roundtable, began meeting that summer. The advisory board chose to expand the statewide clean energy council into a regional, multistate clean energy council, noting that the regional utility grid crossed state borders and regional, multistate solutions would ultimately be most effective. The advisory board also authorized a merger, in a remarkably amicable fashion, with the existing regional, multistate CEO peer support network. This merger not only eliminated duplication but increased access by the council to venture capital funding and CEO peer support resources. Its partner in the merger—the VC-backed CEO network— gained access to the policy reach of the clean energy council. "The targets, and the acceleration initiatives, set the structure for the organization," said the lead organizer.

A new policy committee also began meeting that summer. Its work led, in short order, to a statewide green jobs proposal, marked influence on a new energy bill, and major impact on a global warming solutions act. The act featured, for example, greenhouse gas emission reduction targets set by the stakeholders that day. "We took a very practical approach," said the lead organizer. "Whenever we would lose focus, we would go back to our targets."

A new workforce group organized a Clean Energy Workforce Summit. Four months later, the governor spoke before a different collection of 100 participants, using a substantially similar methodology: four hours, 100 participants, and two big visioning tasks.

The Clean Energy Workforce Summit sought answers to these core questions:

- What are the greatest areas of job opportunity and greatest skill gaps in the clean energy economy? What are the top five?
- What are the most promising acceleration initiatives to meet these opportunities and fill these gaps? What are the top five?

The table work groups, after aggregating their thinking, identified eight key areas of job growth and skill gap:

- Energy auditors: industrial, commercial, and residential.
- Installers/retrofit and conversion (e.g., PV and solar thermal, insulation).
- Technicians: lab, manufacturing, engineering tech.

- Engineers with energy training and energy scientists.
- Green design and construction (e.g., LEED accredited with energy focus).
- Facilities and operations management (e.g., certified energy managers).
- Trainers/educators (industry and academic, credit and noncredit).
- Public communications/education (with energy or sustainability training).

To identify initiatives, the assembled experts rapidly mapped out an action plan with two principal components:

- **Jobs specific.** Clean energy curriculum development for k-12 and higher education, funding for priority initiatives (clean energy jobs bill), low-income community partnership and investment, licensure/certification, jobs demand forecast using multiple inputs (e.g., policy, employers), information clearinghouse for jobs, educational/ training programs, internships and related topics (e.g., career paths).
- **Policy/awareness focused.** Public awareness and civic engagement, upgrade building code/zoning policy to spur demand, align permitting, zoning with global standards and best practices to drive projects.

Clean Energy Council Launches with Support from Diverse Stakeholders

The council was launched. The evaluations from the initial Stakeholders' Roundtable showed that the participants loved not only the process but also the people in the room. People loved the "group activity and the dialogue at the table," the "interaction," and the "open discussion and willingness to listen." They also loved the "good cross section of energy types," the "quality participants," and the "key people in the room." Some complained, not surprisingly, about the tight space and the tight time frames.

The lead organizer reflected:

> The process is concrete and actionable, and I'm a very abstract thinker. But that is why it is so powerful. It is key to jump-starting a process. You're visioning, yes, but you are also taking the next step and putting the vision into action. This way of working is now how we want all our big meetings to be organized. We do it this way now because it distinguishes us from other groups that are less efficient and effective with the time of their members. And an inclusive approach gives us better solutions in the design phase. When we have all the interests at the table, we don't have rework. We hear the objections and factor them in up front. We don't have to go back and get buy-in. We execute faster.

NATURAL FOODS COMPANY RECHARGES IN WAKE OF BUYOUT, MARKET CHANGES

The decade of the 1990s was a time of innovation and growth for many natural foods companies. Before then, many visionary founders had brought quality products to the marketplace but were known primarily to small bands of natural foods consumers. During the 1990s, many of these companies, which had labored largely in obscurity for years, saw their products jump from the small and precious natural foods world to the large and hard-charging mass market.

Success brought new anxieties for these entrepreneurs. In the natural foods hothouse, it was easy for their companies to be small, pure, and good. As mass market companies, they suddenly faced intense pressure to be large, fast, and cheap. For many of these entrepreneurs, success threatened to trigger a massive identity crisis. Would the pure products they lovingly brought into being be compromised by the marketplace? Would the companies they tenaciously built become yet another corporate clone? Would they, literally or figuratively, *sell out?*

One of these companies, representing a premier brand, approached me to lead a visioning session with its senior leadership team as part of its regular quarterly meeting. The morning would be devoted to the numbers, the afternoon to Grounded Visioning. It was a time for the senior people at the company to step back, take stock, reflect on their values, and renew their aspirations.

Good Changes, Great Pressures

The previous year had been challenging. The company had doubled in size. Controlling interest had been sold to a venture capital firm, one of many trolling the natural foods marketplace for new brands and products to inject fast growth into a largely flat industry. The core staff had been retained, but there had been layoffs. There was a change in hierarchy and in structure, but everyone felt the new owners were still focused on the mission and still committed to the company's core values. There was new office space, new products, a new computer system, an injection of capital, and fresh blood, bringing new ideas and energy. In short, lots and lots of change.

Customers' response to the transition had been largely positive, but they were watchful. The staff was cautiously optimistic as well. There was a new sense of things shifting from the informal to the formal and from the fluid to the departmental. Everyone agreed there was more work to do, more pressure, more accountability, and greater uncertainty.

Before beginning the appreciative interviews, I acknowledged all the changes by offering the staff an opportunity to explore their personal relationship with change. I asked them to reflect on the change in the past year and to list aspects that were surprising, positive, and challenging. Next I asked participants to share "crucible" stories, in small groups, that is, difficult personal or professional experiences from which the individual had bounced back and ultimately learned something of lasting value about being resilient in the face of change. Small groups then identified the actions, attitudes, and inner resources that enabled individuals to bounce back. Among the attitudes that emerged, for example, were "resisted initially, followed by letting go" and "focused on the positive." Among the actions taken were "networking continuously" and "quitting what didn't work." Among the inner resources tapped were "finding inner strength" and "having belief in ourselves."

These conversations seemed an appropriate way to allow people to acknowledge the extremely intense experiences that they had lived through recently and to enable them to become present in the moment. There was a sense of owning the past, and drawing some hard-won lessons from it. Fast-growth companies grow so much more rapidly than other organizations that a quarter for them is like a year for most anybody else. These people had packed four years of living into the past 12 months. It had been exhilarating, but tough, and they needed to catch their breath. Not to gripe, but to get a grip.

Exquisite Tension: Growth versus Stability

Having thus set the table, and brought everyone up to the present, we proceeded to introduce the core Grounded Visioning activity. From the question, "What attracted you to this organization, and what keeps you here?" came answers like: "company mission; no bureaucracy; premier brand; corporate culture; social responsibility; flexible, entrepreneurial style."

Asked about high points in their experience of this company, people told stories about visiting an organic wheat harvester and riding a combine and running a promotional event at a ski resort.

The team readily completed the sentence, "When we are at our best, we...," with the following bold assertions, all grounded in their very real stories:

- We are supportive of each other, and we work with the confidence of our leaders.
- We are proud of what we do, are proud of the roles we play, and are passionate about what our brand represents.
- We are excited about our work, our opportunities, our learning, and our achievements.
- We experience opportunity even in a time of scarcity.
- We feel good about our individual skills and see how we make a difference.
- We are committed to growing our company and maintaining the family feel and focus on values that make us who we are.

As team members shared dreams, hopes, and aspirations, a palpable and exquisite tension filled the air. There was a hungry desire to grow rapidly and extensively, fuelled by the investment of the new investors. And there was an equally intense desire to maintain the values and family feel that were perceived to be the "soul" of the company, in the face of that same new investment and ownership.

Aspirations from the former desire included: "Financial reward, streamlined procedures, exceeding expectations, and longevity/fulfilment (grow the company to $100 million and be there to enjoy it!)." Aspirations from the latter desire included: "Make sure this company keeps its soul, maintains the family feel of the company, and makes a positive, lasting impact (from a sustainable brand)."

The day ended with a spontaneous exploration of this "exquisite tension," facing the question, "How can we ensure that we live our mission, remain true to our values, and keep our family feel, as we grow?" The ideas flowed, including the following:

- Live the question continuously, recognizing it as a conflict and a question that never goes away.
- Agree that our values drive our growth, so we should protect and sustain our values.
- Establish indicators for our values and mission and audit progress toward them.
- Keep focus on consumers, who are passionate about product and mission.
- Remember that if we compromise integrity, all we are left with is a commodity.
- Establish system of checks and balances to continually challenge ourselves in a conscious effort (e.g., a socially responsible balanced scorecard).
- Maintain this group since we are committed to values.
- Follow through on ideas for our company that live the mission—letter writing, giving back to communities, volunteerism, food coop, etc.
- Continue to successfully convert to organic—that enables us to support the organic industry and practices while remaining competitive (there is lots of value in organic).
- Remember that just because other companies haven't done it doesn't mean we can't!

This last one was a poignant reminder that many small companies have walked a values-driven path to eventual growth and success, only to lose their "soul" along the way.

A Vision Undone

Indeed, such was the fate, according to those who built it, of the company featured in this case. "It became all about the money," observed a senior manager present that day. "The owners cared about the values only as much as they provided good marketing opportunities. It became more a marketing vehicle than something that was actually practiced."

What happened to the vision created that day? She answered:

> It was a very hopeful moment in time. But then the pressure to perform became phenomenal. They applied it to the CEO, and he applied it to everybody else. Ambitious growth targets were not being met. Attrition started. The CFO was let go, then the CEO. The finances were in disarray. They began to bring in people who were not from the natural or organic world. Ultimately, they shut the headquarters and moved it. Twelve months later, everyone was gone. We were all casualties.

No doubt everyone who participated in the visioning session felt inspired by the results at the time. Yet the aspirations stayed at the high level of values and weren't translated well into operations. Presumably there was an economic case to be made for the company to continue being managed in the way it had been. Presumably there was a way to monetize the contributions of the values that were so important to the employees. If so, the employees failed to make that case and monetize that contribution sufficiently to the company's owners. As a consultant,

I failed to contract to offer enough support after the event to ensure the integration of results with ongoing operations.

In retrospect, there was clearly a disconnect between the employees and their managers and the company's owners and investors. Perhaps this is a situation where we failed to include enough of the "whole system" in the room, and so created a vision that was doomed to fail at winning support from those who did not help create it. It is interesting to imagine how this case might have turned out differently if representatives from owners and investors had been present in the room. In what way might the owners and investors have influenced the employees and managers? And in what way might the employees and managers have influenced the owners and investors?

Instead the two moved forward on separate tracks, not cocreating a future together. In this instance the vision of those who built the company proved incompatible with that of those who ultimately owned it, and those with the controlling interest prevailed.

NOTES

1. Peter Block, "Building Support for Your Vision: Negotiating with Allies and Adversaries," in *The Empowered Manager: Positive Political Skills at Work* (San Francisco: Jossey-Bass, 1987), chap. 5.

2. Peter J. Howe, "Patrick Tries to Kick-Start Energy Tech Industry," *Boston Globe,* June 12, 2007, D.1.

3. Ibid.

PART III

Principles of Grounded Visioning

12

The Power of the Positive

When groups focus on the positive, they see the potential for a better future.

Be not afraid of life. Believe that life is worth living, and your belief will help you create the fact.

—William James

Positive memories serve to awaken the visioning potential of people who participate in a Grounded Visioning session.

Coming to an understanding of how groups create shared realities is not merely an academic exercise. Good practice is informed by good theory. This chapter shows the connection between two theories—"social constructionism" and "appreciative inquiry"—and the practical reasons for focusing on the positive in a Grounded Visioning session.

SOCIAL CONSTRUCTIONISM AND THE ROLE OF LANGUAGE

"Social constructionism" is the idea that what we consider to be the "truth" upon which we act is not inherent in events themselves but rather is created in our conversations about what those events signify. That means that if we describe an event in positive terms—an amazing 50 percent of members attended the meeting—we define the event as a success. If we speak in negative terms—can you believe 50 percent of people could not bother to attend—we get a completely different picture of the same event.

Here's a short anecdote that shows us social constructionism at the ballpark:

Three umpires are discussing the calling of strikes and balls. The first one, speaking strictly from an objective perspective, says: "There's strikes and then there's balls, and I calls 'em like they is." The second one, having grasped the subtlety of what we might call the subjective perspective, says: "There's strikes and then there's balls, and I calls 'em like I sees 'em." The third umpire, speaking from the perspective of a social constructionist, announces: "There's only pitches, and those pitches ain't nothin' till I calls 'em!"

In this anecdote, the different descriptions of calling balls and strikes reflect different views of reality. The umpires make us wonder just where the streaking blurred pitch ends and the reality created by the umpires' words—and affirmed by listening fans—begins.

"Truth" Is an Agreement among People

The central theorists of social constructionism claim that what we accept as reality and progress is actually socially constructed between us and not founded in "truth" or inherent to any objective world separate from our attachment of meaning to it. In other words, we create the world we inhabit, and we do so principally through language and conversation.

Some practitioners extend this observation to suggest that organizations exist not only in their tangible trappings—their computers, buildings, and patents, for example—or even in their people (who may come and go) but also in the conversations of people who believe in the organization and commit to renew it. Through their ideas, beliefs, and commitments expressed in conversation, the theory goes, the organization is born, functions, and is renewed. Without those life-giving conversations, the organization ceases to exist.

Implications for Grounded Visioning

What does this mean for Grounded Visioning? Grounded Visioning is very sensitive to the power of language. Social constructionism doesn't tell us that conversation about the future creates a future that exists in another time and place, waiting for us. It says that having conversations about our envisioned future actually creates that future now, in the moment we commit to bring it about.

Consider this famous quotation, commonly attributed to Goethe but actually written by the Scottish mountaineer William Hutchinson Murray in 1951:[1]

Until one is committed, there is hesitancy, the chance to draw back. Concerning all acts of initiative (and creation), there is one elementary truth, the ignorance of which kills countless ideas and splendid plans: that the moment one definitely commits oneself, then Providence moves too. All sorts of things occur to help one that would never otherwise have occurred. A whole stream of events issues from the decision, raising in one's favor all manner of unforeseen incidents and meetings and material assistance, which no man could have dreamed would have come his way. Whatever you can do, or dream you can do, begin it. Boldness has genius, power, and magic in it. Begin it now.

Bringing a shared vision of the future into focus creates clarity of purpose and enthusiasm for action that can lead to seemingly miraculous results. Consider again, the case of the Arts and Crafts Guild, described in Chapter 2. The Guild's vision, which emerged in just about three hours, coalesced into a vivid commitment to create a signature crafts fair. Once this image of the future became clear, it was obvious and compelling to all that the Guild should create it. A long-standing but fuzzy competing alternative—that of being some kind of museum—immediately fell away. So compelling was the vision that it was brought into reality in nine months—half the time that is normally required for such an ambitious undertaking. Viewed from this perspective—that of the social construction of reality—one sees that the Guild actually created its new future that night and rapidly grew into it over the following months.

APPRECIATIVE INQUIRY AND THE IMAGINATION

Appreciative Inquiry is a revolutionary approach to management, leadership, and organization development born out of social constructionism and defined by the authors Jane Watkins and Bernard Mohr in *Appreciative Inquiry: Change at the Speed of Imagination.*[2]

> Appreciative Inquiry [is] a theory and practice for approaching change from a holistic framework. Based on the belief that human systems are made and imagined by those who live and work within them, AI leads systems to move toward the generative and creative images that reside in their most positive core—their values, visions, achievements, and best practices. AI is both a world view and a practical process. In theory, AI is a perspective, a set of principles and beliefs about how human systems function, a departure from the past metaphor of human systems as machines...In practice, AI can be used to co-create the transformative processes and practices appropriate to the culture of a particular organization...Grounded in the theory of "social constructionism," AI recognizes that human systems are constructions of the imagination and are, therefore, capable of change at the speed of imagination.

By "inquiry" we mean the process of seeking to understand through asking questions. The term "appreciative" comes from two ideas—that when something increases in value it "appreciates." And when we appreciate something, its value to us increases by our recognition. Therefore, Appreciative Inquiry begins by studying the generative and life-giving forces in the system—the things we want to increase—and then translating that knowledge into organizational innovation.

"Problems" Are the Problem

Mohr and Watkins tell the story of the method's origins:[3]

> AI first arose in the early 1980s, when David Cooperrider, then a graduate student at Case Western Reserve University, was hired to conduct an organizational diagnosis of

the Cleveland Clinic to find out what was wrong with the way the organization was operating. During his research, he was amazed by the level of cooperation, innovation, and egalitarian governance that he observed within certain parts of the medical facility. In response to these observations, Cooperrider refocused his research to study the causes of such excellence. He soon found that this "appreciative" approach was causing a powerful and creative stir within the organization. As he began to formalize a theory based on his findings, clinic leaders asked him to help them create a practice based on positive inquiry. Soon Cooperrider began to see broader possibilities for applying this emerging philosophy to guide change in other organizations.

David Cooperrider came to realize, as he writes in *Lessons from the Field:*[4]

[Appreciative Inquiry] deliberately seeks to discover people's exceptionality—their unique gifts, strengths, and qualities. It actively searches and recognizes people for their specialties—their essential contributions and achievements. And it is based on principles of equality of voice—everyone is asked to speak about their vision of the true, the good, and the possible. Appreciative Inquiry builds momentum and success because it believes in people. It really is an invitation to a positive revolution. Its goal is to discover in all human beings the exceptional and the essential. Its goal is to create organizations that are in full voice!

Mohr and Watkins further detail the principles from which Appreciative Inquiry derives its power:[5]

- **The constructionist principle.** Our organizations evolve in the direction of the images we create based on the questions we ask as we strive to understand the systems at work.
- **The principle of simultaneity.** Change begins the moment we ask questions.
- **The anticipatory principle.** Our behavior in the present is influenced by the future we anticipate.
- **The poetic principle.** Just as poets have no constraints on what they can write about, we have no boundaries on what we can inquire and learn from.
- **The positive principle.** The more positive the questions used to guide a change process, the more long-lasting and effective that process will be.

These principles are in play in the unabashedly positive questions that spark and animate the Grounded Visioning process.

Positive Thinking Affects Outcomes

David Cooperrider recounts six extensive areas of research that support a vibrant link between "positive imagery and positive action,"[6] including these two popularly recognized phenomena:

- The placebo response, "in which projected images, as reflected in positive belief in the efficacy of a remedy, ignite a healing response that can be every bit as powerful as conventional therapy."[7]

- The Pygmalion effect, in which a positive image of another "plants a seed that redi-
rects the mind of the perceiver to think about and see the other with affirmative
eyes,"[8] thus bringing about a self-fulfilling prophecy.

Grounded Visioning aligns itself with these powerful and emerging understandings that tell us, as Cooperrider concludes, that "we are each made and imagined
in the eyes of one another."[9]

Appreciative Inquiry Summits: Another Approach to Visioning

Appreciative Inquiry has given rise to its own remarkable, large group visioning process known as the Appreciative Inquiry Summit, elegantly described in a
book of the same name.[10] Typically, the AI Summit spans three to five consecu-
tive days. It brings anywhere from 50 to 500 or more people together to:

- Discover the organization or community's core competencies and strengths.
- Envision opportunities for positive change.
- Design the desired changes into the organization or community's systems, structures,
strategies, and culture.
- Implement and sustain the change and make it work.

The AI Summit is a radical shift away from traditional change management
approaches that put the responsibility for change in the hands of just a few individuals and are based on the assumption that the best way to move forward is to
solve problems. The AI Summit assumes that organizations change fastest and
best when their members are excited about where they are going, have a clear
plan for moving forward, and feel confident about their ability to reach their destination. In other words, quick and effective organization change is a product of

---

Learn More...

About Social Construction

An Invitation to Social Construction by Kenneth J. Gergen (Thousand Oaks, CA: Sage
Publications, 1999).
Social Construction: Entering the Dialogue by Kenneth J. Gergen and Mary Gergen
(Taos, NM: Taos Institute Publications, 2004).

About Appreciative Inquiry

Appreciative Inquiry: Change at the Speed of Imagination by Jane Magruder Watkins and
Bernard J. Mohr (San Francisco: Jossey-Bass, 2001).
The Essentials of Appreciative Inquiry: A Roadmap for Creating Positive Futures
(Waltham, MA: Pegasus Communications, 2002).
http://appreciativeinquiry.case.edu/.

having the "whole system" aligned around its strengths and around ideas that generate energy for action.

The AI Summit was initially conceived in the mid-1980s and has, over the years, incorporated key elements of other large group process methodologies, including Real Time Strategic Change,[11] Open Space Technology,[12] and Future Search Conferences.[13] It has become a popular means for accelerating change by involving a broad range of internal and external stakeholders in a fully positive and narrative-based change process that involves not only inquiry and visioning but also design and implementation planning. For organizations with time, this is an excellent visioning process.

Implications for Grounded Visioning

The theory of Appreciative Inquiry informs the practice of Grounded Visioning in several ways:

- The faith in the goodness of people and the positive core of every organization embodied throughout the practice of Grounded Visioning.
- The promise of questioning as a means to awaken a sense of vitality and that positive core in groups, quickly.
- The actual wording of those questions as an efficient means to access that vitality and positive core.

Recall, for example, the emotions motivating the Nonprofit Summit in Chapter 9. A whole sector composed of dedicated, hardworking, competent, and mission-driven people had recently come under political fire for mismanagement. People were frustrated and angry at the perceived injustice. That emotion running strong among a gathering of 250 people could easily have led to a blustery session filled with blame, counterattacks, and venting.

With the very first activity, likely seen by most as merely a means to break the ice, individuals at their tables shared high point stories of their experience working in the nonprofit sector. Out poured story after story after story of courage, contribution, sacrifice, creativity, and leadership. The whole atmosphere of the room changed dramatically. People connected with their pride and their commitment. They touched their deepest values and strongest beliefs. They felt their positive core and saw and heard it in others, and it inspired them. From that place, everything that emerged was positive, constructive, and dynamic. The practice of Appreciative Inquiry creates the fertile field from which the Grounded Vision emerges.

NOTES

1. William Hutchinson Murray, *The Scottish Himalayan Expedition* (London: Dent, 1951), http://german.about.com/library/blgermyth12.htm (accessed May 28, 2008).

2. Jane Watkins and Bernard Mohr, *Appreciative Inquiry: Change at the Speed of Imagination* (San Francisco: Jossey-Bass, 2001), xxxi–xxxii.

3. Bernard J. Mohr and Jane Magruder Watkins, *The Essentials of Appreciative Inquiry: A Roadmap for Creating Positive Futures,* Innovations in Management Series (Waltham, MA: Pegasus Communications, 2002), 2.

4. Sue Annis Hammond and Cathy Royal, *Lessons from the Field—Applying Appreciative Inquiry* (Bend, OR: Thin Book Publishing, 2001), 12.

5. Mohr and Watkins, *The Essentials of Appreciative Inquiry,* 5.

6. David L. Cooperrider, "Positive Image, Positive Action: The Affirmative Basis of Organizing," in David L. Cooperrider, Peter F. Sorenson Jr., Diana Whitney, and Therese F. Yaeger, eds., *Appreciative Inquiry: Rethinking Human Organization Toward a Positive Theory of Change* (Champaign, IL: Stipes Publishing, 1999), chap. 2.

7. Ibid.

8. Ibid.

9. Ibid.

10. James D. Ludema, Diana Whitney, Bernard J. Mohr, and Thomas J. Griffin, *The Appreciative Inquiry Summit—A Practitioner's Guide for Leading Large-Group Change* (San Francisco: Berrett-Koehler, 2003).

11. For information on this remarkable process, see Robert J. Jacobs, *Real Time Strategic Change* (San Francisco: Berrett-Koehler, 1994).

12. See Harrison Owen, *Open Space Technology: A User's Guide* (San Francisco: Berrett-Koehler, 1997).

13. Marvin R. Weisbord and Sandra Janoff, *Future Search: An Action Guide to Finding Common Ground in Organizations & Communities* (San Francisco: Berrett-Koehler, 1995).

—— 13 ——

The Genius of the Group

Better decisions come from involving all stakeholders.

What lies behind us and what lies before us are tiny matters compared to what lies within us.

—Ralph Waldo Emerson

W hy should we trust the future of organizations to the people who work in them, rather than relying solely on the talent and wisdom of leaders who have risen to the top of their ranks? Don't leaders have the knowledge and perspective to make choices for organizations?

For example, we don't trust people to take responsibility for their own medical care. We entrust our health to highly trained doctors, who make the diagnosis and prescribe the treatment. We don't trust insiders to know better than consultants when change needs to happen. Most consulting dollars go to experts who diagnose problems, make recommendations, and then leave.

But, in fact, research on patient safety errors routinely shows that nurses, or other members of the medical staff, and patients can prevent errors if they would have the confidence to speak up—trusting their own expertise as well as that of the most credentialed expert.[1] And many businesspeople can tell stories of expert consultants who imposed solutions on work groups without considering all the knowledge that insiders had amassed. Despite expert knowledge and careful analysis, the resulting solution solved the wrong problem or solved the right problem in the wrong way or just never quite got implemented. Even in your own household, I'm sure you can think of instances where an authoritarian "because I said so" led to choices later regretted.

So while top-down decisions may be necessary in some situations, in most instances, you can trust people with their own futures. While it may seem radical, you can trust people to know what is best, even for themselves.

This is what we do in Grounded Visioning. We trust people because, collectively, they do know best. Much scholarly research supports this idea.

NONEXPERTS ARE CAPABLE OF GREAT INSIGHT

In the mid twentieth century, organizers took a much more hierarchical and exclusive approach to meeting design. Even among organizational psychologists, it was assumed that participants in a meeting needed to be guided and led like schoolchildren.

Like many discoveries, the insight about the wisdom of trusting people began with an accident. Kurt Lewin, the German-born psychologist recognized by many as the founder of social psychology, directed a conference on race relations in New Britain, Connecticut in 1946.[2] He enlisted the help of three small group facilitators: Kenneth Benne, Leland Bradford, and Ronald Lippitt. The three facilitators led participants through a variety of self-disclosing activities and challenges each day. A research staff member assigned to each group made observations about the participants and shared them in nightly debriefing sessions. Every night, the leaders and their assistants would gather to process what they had observed and what they had learned. It was presumed that the real, deep learning about what was taking place each day would be revealed during these evening sessions by those who knew best.

News spread about these sessions. One evening, three participants—nonexperts—asked to attend. Lewin, with his brilliant and curious mind, agreed.

Figure 13.1
Group decision-making is good decision-making: Collectively, people do know best.

Illustration by Cindy Murphy.

What he learned astonished him. He found that participants were capable of deep self-reflection, insight, and telling peer feedback. They could be in charge of their own learning and serve in the learning of others.

The expert—Lewin—learned to trust the people in the room and placed this formative imprint on many of his future contributions to the field of applied social psychology. Not surprisingly, the participants in that conference were excited by the experience. The next night—and every night thereafter—every participant joined the evening debriefing session for animated conversation.

Today, we credit Lewin, acknowledged as the father of social psychology, for the insights that began to show the importance of group dynamics. We celebrate his humility as someone who learned from practice and experience, as captured in his comment, "If you want to understand something, try to change it." Lewin also used data and feedback to change behavior, similar to the way the Grounded Visioning uses past successes to inspire dreams for the future.

Planning Become Inclusive

Lewin's insights influenced two innovative meeting facilitators on opposite sides of the Atlantic Ocean: Ron Lippitt in the United States and Eric Trist in England.

Following up on the successful accident of 1946, Lewin organized a conference that formally included participants' giving and receiving feedback about their own behavior and that of others in groups. This first training conference that featured participants' feedback on their own behavior as a core design element was held in 1947 in Bethel, Maine.[3] Called the National Training Laboratory in Group Dynamics, it led to the founding of NTL Institute, which has since been a source of innovation and training for new views of organizations and new tools for working with them.

The NTL Institute's faculty, including Ron Lippitt, began expanding the boundaries of small group work by convening large training conferences on higher education change in the late 1950s and 1960s.[4] Their purpose was to train faculty and staff from colleges and universities during two-week sessions to introduce change back into their home institutions. The staff working with these conferences began to learn how to manage the dynamics of meetings of 100 participants or more.

Lippitt went on to introduce two striking innovations in organizational practice.[5] First, he questioned the consulting profession's focus on solving problems, observing with frustration that it caused a profound drain in an organization's energy for making change. Instead he engaged diverse stakeholders in envisioning their "preferred future," observing that such action mobilized tremendous positive energy and excitement.[6] Then, along with fellow NTL trainer Eva Schindler-Rainman, he began introducing this "preferred future visioning" method to large numbers of community activists, sometimes convening hundreds of participants.[7]

Successful Meetings Get Larger and Larger

Kathleen Dannemiller and others extended Lippitt's work "into mainstream corporate America through the use of five-day interactive working sessions for up to 200 participants at Ford Motor Company."[8] Dannemiller Tyson Associates became acknowledged masters at "changing the way change occurs" by developing principles and practices for engaging large groups in creating rapid change. For example, I assisted Kathleen Dannemiller in facilitating a three-day change conference of a whole university system with 350 participants.

Many of the principles vital to the success of Lippitt's work appear in Dannemiller's, now applied to larger groups and corporate settings:

- Whole system in the room.
- Common database from participants.
- Dialogue, not problem solving, as the norm.
- Round table work groups in "max-mix" groupings of stakeholders.
- Self-managing work groups using handouts and worksheets.

English Counterparts Create First "Search Conference"

Lewin also inspired Eric Trist, who helped found the Tavistock Institute for Human Relations, the English counterpart to the NTL Institute, in 1947, and who worked on the interaction of social and technical factors in organizations.[9] Trist's colleague, the Australian academic Fred Emery, joined him in seeking "new ways to engage larger, more complex organizations and social systems in processes of learning that would lead to change."[10] Their joint pursuits led them to design the first "search conference" in 1960.[11]

This first search conference was a creative response to a mandate by the government to bring together Britain's two aircraft engine makers. Their study conference, engaging participants and expert speakers, examined global forces, industry trends, and the company context to set the stage for participants to collectively conceive of a joint future together. Emery, and later with his wife Merrelyn, went on to lead hundreds of these sessions around the world.[12] Their preferred working group was 32 individuals.

Finding Common Ground Becomes Easy, Predictable

As Dannemiller was inspired by Lippitt to extend his work into new and larger arenas, so Marvin Weisbord was inspired by both Emery[13] and Lippitt[14] to break new ground, and thus create the Future Search Conference.[15] The Future Search Conference is a powerful methodology for discovering common ground among large, diverse groups of stakeholders. Future Search Conferences typically require two and one half days, and are limited to 64 invited participants, at eight tables of 8.

Thus the two large group processes that most shape the Grounded Visioning process, at least as it scales to large group sizes, are Weisbord's work with Future Search Conferences (with group sizes that tend to cap out at 64) and Dannemiller's work with Real Time Strategic Change, now known as Whole Scale Change (with group sizes that tend to start where the Future Search Conference leaves off). Grounded Visioning draws inspiration from both in how it aims to find common ground among diverse participants by engaging them in creating community and in vibrantly envisioning the future.

When you lead a large group version of a Grounded Visioning session, you will use process innovations that lead back through time from Weisbord and Dannemiller (I trained with both) to Lippitt, Emery, Trist, and Lewin. These include the following:

- Getting as much of the whole system (all the stakeholders who have a stake in the future of the team, company, organization, or community) in the room as possible.
- Designing much of the work to be done in self-managed teams at tables working in parallel, guided by handouts and worksheets.
- Building a common database from the expertise of the stakeholders in the room, not experts from outside speaking at the participants.
- Striving to find common ground, focusing on what people want, and not on solving problems.
- Ending with a focus on action and implementation.

Large Group Meetings Become the New Norm

Grounded Visioning makes it possible for hundreds of people to collaboratively define an organization's vision. People frequently use Grounded Visioning because it scales up so well to large groups.

Intuitively, leaders know that if you want to create a shared vision, it makes sense to get everyone together in the same room. But this insight is not just common sense. A number of academics and researchers have showed that large group decision-making not only leads to better decisions but also makes implementation faster, more efficient, and more successful.

Barbara Benedict Bunker and Billie T. Alban cataloged the benefits of "large group interventions" in their landmark special issue of the *Journal of Applied Behavioral Science* in 1992:[16]

- The greater speed of change that comes from involving everyone at once allows a more rapid response to global competition than the more traditional, top-down, trickle-down form of change.
- The greater impact on people and culture in the organization that comes from being in the same room, hearing the same information, sharing the same experience, and arriving at the same conclusions about the future allows a more effective response to changing conditions.

Learn More...

Strategic Change

Real Time Strategic Change by Robert J. Jacobs (San Francisco: Berrett-Koehler, 1994).
Whole Scale Change—Tools for Unleashing the Magic in Organizations by Dannemiller
   Tyson Associates (San Francisco: Berrett-Koehler, 2000).
www.dannemillertyson.com.

Future Search

Future Search: An Action Guide to Finding Common Ground in Organizations &
   Communities by Marvin R. Weisbord and Sandra Janoff (San Francisco: Berrett-
   Koehler, 1995).
www.futuresearch.net.

Working with Large Groups

Large Group Interventions: Engaging the Whole System for Rapid Change by Barbara
   Benedict Bunker and Billie T. Alban (San Francisco, CA: Jossey-Bass, 1996).

Organizational Change Methodologies

The Change Handbook: The Definitive Handbook on Today's Best Methods for Engaging
   Whole Systems by Peggy Holman, Tom Devane, and Steven Cady (San Francisco,
   CA: Berrett-Koehler, 2007).

- The greater opportunity for emerging leadership to surface, engage, and step forward that comes from authentic, widespread participation allows a wider sense of ownership and accountability for implementing the vision.
- The greater exchange of ideas between levels and functions within an organization, and stakeholders in and out of an organization, that comes from actively engaging maximum diversity leads to greater empathy and better solutions.
- The greater perspective that individuals gain about the whole organization that comes from experiencing "the whole," perhaps for the first time, allows for more globally informed action to happen at the local level when taking next steps.

For these reasons, it is now common that many meeting methods scale to work at the level of hundreds of participants. That has not always been the case, and I am grateful for the social innovators who helped make it so.

CROWDS CAN BE WISE

James Surowiecki recently gave us a new and even deeper understanding of the genius of groups with his 2004 book, *The Wisdom of Crowds—Why the Many*

Are Smarter than the Few and How Collective Wisdom Shapes Business, Economies, Societies, and Nations. He explains how, "under the right circumstances, groups are remarkably intelligent, and are often smarter than the smartest people in them." Going further, he adds, "Even if most of the people within a group are not especially well-informed or rational, it can still reach a collectively wise decision."[17]

What are the special circumstances that give rise to such an extraordinary "collective wisdom?" Surowiecki's research reveals four conditions that characterize wise crowds:[18]

- Diversity of opinion (each person should have some private information, even if it's just an eccentric interpretation of the known facts),
- Independence (people's opinions are not determined by the opinions of those around them),
- Decentralization (people are able to specialize and draw on local knowledge), and
- Aggregation (some mechanism exists for turning private judgments into a collective decision).

A group that satisfies these conditions is likely to make accurate judgments, Surowiecki writes.

He explains:

Why? At heart, the answer rests on a mathematical truism. If you ask a large enough group of diverse, independent people to make a prediction or estimate of a probability, and then average those estimates, the errors each of them makes in coming up with an answer will cancel themselves out. Each person's guess, you might say, has two components, information and error. Subtract the error, and you're left with the information.[19]

Implications for Grounded Visioning

Let's view Grounding Visioning through the lens of the four conditions that enable groups to "subtract the error" and be "left with the information." In each instance, we will consider the case of a large urban community college convening a visioning session among 250 participants and how their gathering tapped the wisdom of the crowd.

Diversity, Surowiecki's first condition, is an essential aspect of the Grounded Visioning large group design. Right up front, the planning committee is charged to bring the "whole system" into the room. Diversity of views is an explicit planning goal. Grounded Visioning ensures that diverse viewpoints will be heard by making sure people with different priorities, backgrounds, and roles are included. Assigned seating further ensures a diversity of views at every table in the room. Finally, the meeting leaders offer explicit ground rules to ensure a fair hearing of divergent views. At a Grounded Visioning session, there are no experts to tell participants what they should think.

This community college invited 125 internal participants (faculty, staff, administrators, board members, and students) and 125 external participants (alumni, neighbors, community leaders, educators, and business leaders). Seating was assigned to ensure diversity at every table.

Independence, the second condition, is a highly valued component of the large group process. The group's eventual vision is built from data that come from individuals sharing high point stories and their dreams, hopes, and aspirations. The data collection process is structured so that each individual is able to share his or her story—his or her independent contribution—without interruption. The process pauses for individuals to share their dreams, hopes, and aspirations in private pairs in order to preserve as much of their independence of thought as possible. As Surowiecki observes, "Paradoxically the best way for a group to be smart is for each person to think and act as independently as possible."[20]

At the college visioning session, every individual had an opportunity to share his or her dreams, hopes, and aspirations for the college with peers at the table. Every person had a private moment to reflect on what they wanted most for the institution and to share it in an atmosphere informed by the ground rule, "all ideas are valid."

Grounded Visioning relies on **decentralization,** Surowiecki's third condition, to make it possible to hear everyone in a large group. Work is distributed among tables of eight. The meeting leader delegates to these groups important responsibilities for self-management. Decentralization of authority into small work groups brings a heightened sense of engagement to every participant. With a greater sense of autonomy comes the expectation of higher performance. As Surowiecki observes, "The more responsibility people have for their own environments, the more engaged they will be."[21]

In addition, decentralization dampens the effect of dysfunctional behavior. If you are worried about a loud and loquacious few who monologue and harangue, the large group is spared this horror partly by distributing the large group's work to smaller, decentralized work groups, where the effect of such individuals can be localized and minimized.

Also, when you distribute work among a number of groups, the best thinking will appear again and again. It will be easy to see the strong ideas when the groups' work is aggregated.

The community college seated participants at more than 30 tables of eight to ensure that a great many conversations could happen in parallel. It gave each table the opportunity to choose its own leadership roles such as facilitator, recorder, timekeeper, and reporter so as to assume greater responsibility and autonomy for its work. It gave each table the same task so that the common ground thinking would emerge over and over again throughout the room.

Surowiecki sees **aggregation,** the fourth condition, as key:

> An intelligent group, especially when confronted with cognition problems, does not ask its members to modify their positions in order to let the group reach a decision

everyone can be happy with. Instead it figures out how to use mechanisms—like market prices, or intelligent voting systems—to aggregate and produce collective judgments that represent not what any one person in the group thinks but rather, in some sense, what they all think.[22]

The Grounded Visioning large group process uses aggregation in four ways:

- Aggregating the common themes of the high point stories.
- Aggregating the common themes of the dreams, hopes, and aspirations shared by individuals in pairs.
- Aggregating the common themes of the dreams, hopes, and aspirations shared by the table groups at the Vision Wall.
- Aggregating the multi-votes of the entire group to identify the most engaging dreams, hopes, and aspirations for the group as a whole (Surowiecki would call multi-voting an "intelligent voting system").

These aggregation methods, by compiling "what any one person in the group thinks," give us, ultimately, "what they all think." Facilitators sometimes call this the sense of the group. People who work with groups a great deal can feel it. Aggregation removes the need to have the intuition to recognize the sense of the group. Instead, the data methodically reveal the sense of the group.

Lastly, the community college aggregated data in the four ways listed above, capturing the aspirations of the individuals in the room, as filtered by their work groups, on a huge wide Vision Wall at the front of the room. As a result it was able to distill the best thinking of 250 busy leaders and stakeholders into a set of shared goals in just half a day. These goals served the college well as guides for the next several years.

A FINAL WORD

Even if you still have the nagging feeling that the executives of your organization really do know best, there's another reason to invite more people into the decision-making process: People support what they help create. If you are a leader who wants followers, listen to where your people want to go. MIT's Peter Senge writes:

But many leaders have personal visions that never get translated into shared visions that galvanize an organization...What has been lacking is a discipline for translating vision into shared vision...In mastering this discipline, leaders learn the counter-productiveness of trying to dictate a vision, no matter how heartfelt.[23]

Fast forward to a coaching session with a community college president. She is staking the success of her presidency on a college-wide visioning session, with more than 100 invited outsiders, at which the goals for the future of the college for the next three years will be discussed and decided. I ask her, "Is anything a given here? Is anything off the table here? Are you comfortable allowing this large group to set a direction that you must implement, not knowing what that might be?" She responds, "We have a tremendous amount to do here at the college. I trust this group to know what needs to be done. And if it is not exactly what I would choose, it is what they have the passion to accomplish, and so we will get it done faster, and then move on to other things that I might want more. Ultimately, I trust that my agenda, and that of this group of committed advisors, will find lots of common ground." And so she trusted. We entered the session with no preset givens, and with nothing off the table. This president has become one of the most productive and effective leaders with whom I have worked.

Why do we trust people, and the genius of groups? Because it works.

NOTES

1. See A. C. Edmondson, "Learning from Mistakes Is Easier Said Than Done: Group and Organizational Influences on the Detection and Correction of Human Error," *Journal of Applied Behavioral Science* 32, no. 1 (1996): 5. A. C. Edmondson, "Psychological Safety and Learning Behavior in Work Teams," *Administrative Science Quarterly* 44, no. 2 (1999): 350–83. I. M. Nembhard and A. C. Edmondson, "Making It Safe: The Effects of Leader Inclusiveness and Professional Status on Psychological Safety and Improvement Efforts in Health Care Teams," *Journal of Organizational Behavior* 27, no. 7 (2006): 941.

2. See Marshall Scott Poole and Andrea B. Hollingshead, *Theories of Small Groups: Interdisciplinary Perspectives* (Thousand Oaks, CA: Sage Publications, 2005), 73–74. See also www.ntl.org (accessed May 28, 2008).

3. Ibid., 74.

4. Barbara Benedict Bunker and Billie T. Alban, "Large Group Intervention—A New Social Innovation?" *Journal of Applied Behavioral Science* 28, no. 4, Special Issue: Large Group Interventions (December 1992): 475.

5. Kathleen D. Dannemiller and Robert W. Jacobs, "Changing the Way Organizations Change: A Revolution of Common Sense," *Journal of Applied Behavioral Science* 28, no. 4, Special Issue: Large Group Interventions (December 1992): 481–82.

6. Ronald Lippitt, "Future Before You Plan," in *NTL Manager's Handbook* (Arlington, VA: NTL Institute, 1983).

7. Eva Schindler-Rainman and Ronald Lippitt, *Building the Collaborative Community: Mobilizing Citizens for Action* (Irvine, CA: University of California, 1980).

8. Dannemiller and Jacobs, "Changing the Way Organizations Change," 482.

9. Eric Trist and W. Bamforth, "Some Social and Psychological Consequences of the Long Wall Method of Coal-Getting," *Human Relations* 4 (1951): 3–38.

10. William Pasmore, "Biography of Fred Emery," *Journal of Applied Behavioral Science* 28, no. 4, Special Issue: Large Group Interventions (December 1992): 472.

11. Marvin R. Weisbord and others, *Discovering Common Ground* (San Francisco: Berrett-Koehler, 1992), 19–33.

12. Merrelyn Emery, ed., *Participative Design for Participative Democracy* (Canberra: Centre for Continuing Education, Australian National University, 1993).

13. Marvin R. Weisbord, "Future Search," in *Productive Workplaces: Organizing and Managing for Dignity, Meaning and Community* (San Francisco: Jossey-Bass, 1987), chap. 14.

14. Marvin R. Weisbord and Sandra Janoff, *Future Search: An Action Guide to Finding Common Ground in Organizations & Communities* (San Francisco: Berrett-Koehler, 1995), 12.

15. Weisbord and others, *Discovering Common Ground;* and Weisbord and Janoff, *Future Search.*

16. Barbara Benedict Bunker and Billie T. Alban, "Conclusion: What Makes Large Group Interventions Effective?" *Journal of Applied Behavioral Science* 28, no. 4, Special Issue: Large Group Interventions (December 1992): 579.

17. James Surowiecki, *The Wisdom of Crowds—Why the Many Are Smarter than the Few and How Collective Wisdom Shapes Business, Economies, Societies, and Nations* (New York: Doubleday, 2004), xiii.

18. Ibid., 10.

19. Ibid.

20. Ibid., xix.

21. Ibid., 212.

22. Ibid., xix.

23. Peter M. Senge, *The Fifth Discipline. The Art and Practice of the Learning Organization* (London: Random House, 1990), 9.

—————— 14 ——————

The Spark of Sight

People can handle lots of information when they think with both words and pictures.

The visual approach has a special power for seeing patterns and solving problems.
—Thomas West[1]

P articipants often come up to me after Grounded Visioning sessions and say, "I'm a very visual person. I'm so glad you work the way that you do. It makes everything so easy for me to follow."
Grounded Visioning method is effective because participants visualize much of the information with which they work. We use lists and clusters. We remind ourselves with display boards. We don't just talk about connections; we see them.

PICTURES REALLY ARE WORTH A THOUSAND WORDS

This reflects the growing understanding that we can think differently when information is presented visually. Edward Tufte, a graphics designer and professor at Princeton University, has shown how important pictures are for analysis and decision-making in situations as different as understanding the underlying causes of Napoleon's disastrous retreat from Moscow and seeing how available information could have prevented the Challenger space shuttle disaster in 1986.[2]

Educators, scientists, and technologists have put into practice methods that tap into the power of visual presentation of information. Elementary school students, for example, have moved away from Roman numeral style outlining to more visual brainstorming tools that incorporate proximity, colors, words written in different sizes, pictures, arrows, circles, and connecting lines to organize their thoughts. Anna Adam and Helen Mowers write in *School Library Journal,* "Graphic representations of ideas and how they connect to each other can help students through that brainstorming process, helping them organize their thoughts in a visual, nonlinear way before taking pen to paper (or fingers to keyboard)."[3]

Too Much Data? Make a Picture

But pictures and visualization are not just for kindergarten. Government and businesses increasingly use graphical methods to gain insights into massive amounts of data. The Department of Homeland Security, for example, sponsors the National Visual Analytics Center, which aims to develop means to visually represent large amounts of data.[4]

Many software companies are working in the new field of "visual analytics" to help humans take in and gain insights from vast amounts of computer-generated data. The web site of an organizing tool called the Axon idea processor, for example, maintains: "The visual cortex (or hind-brain) has evolved over 100 million years to become a massively parallel device. In contrast, the logical front-brain has only 1 million years of evolution, dating back to the ape man. Hence our vision is by far the more efficient and powerful of the faculties."[5]

With the data explosion created by powerful computers, visual methods increasingly find their way into technical disciplines. Seth Lloyd, a professor of mechanical engineering at MIT, interviewed at www.edge.org, notes the limits of nongraphical representations: "It even turns out that if you rely on language as the sole interface for computers, people can't use them once they grow beyond a certain scale, and we crossed that boundary in our Moore's Law-paced engineering adventures about a decade ago. Now we must rely on visual/spatial interfaces mixed with linguistic ones."[6]

Visual Principles and the World Wide Web

Online, you can see these principles at work in web search engines like Grokker (www.grokker.com) and tools like the visual thesaurus (www.visualthesaurus.com). These use visual presentation to help people see patterns, make connections, and rank choices. "Grokker divides results into categories that are displayed as circles containing subcategories in smaller circles or squares. Clicking on any circle or square expands the shape to show its contents."[7] The visual thesaurus uses color and proximity to visually depict the relationships among words.

Another example of the power of pictures to support analytical thought is Newsmap, which visually depicts the patterns in news reporting. Newsmap (http://www.marumushi.com/apps/newsmap/index.cfm) uses color and size to show type of news and volume of reporting, respectively.

Via Pictures, Learn and Organize Quickly

These visualization techniques are based on the "cognitive theory that many people more easily learn and recall information through graphical representations."[8] Many build on the ideas of Tony Buzan, who in the 1960s developed his "mind mapping" technique.[9]

Thomas West, who has explored links among creativity, visual thinking, and dyslexia and other learning problems, writes that "historically, some of the most original thinkers in fields ranging from physical science and mathematics to politics and poetry have relied heavily on visual modes of thought."[10]

West writes, "the literature on creativity has long observed that the most important thing is *seeing* the big patterns and *seeing* the unexpected connections and novel solutions."[11]

This is why, in Grounded Visioning, we use our eyes to process information: because they help us see big patterns and novel solutions. While using more than one sense may seem like common sense, it is anything but common in modern meetings.

THE INSPIRATION FOR THE VISUAL IN GROUNDED VISIONING

The inspiration for the essential visual practice underlying Grounded Visioning came on a remote mountain slope in the Himalayas in 1963. Jiro Kawakita had a problem he couldn't solve. Kawakita, a cultural anthropologist, was on an expedition to Nepal, to study the culture of rice-cultivating peoples in Southeast Asia. He had visited this group of five mountainside villages twice before in the previous decade, once attached as a scientist to a climbing expedition and once for purely scientific research. He had fallen in love with this distant place and its remarkable people living in a valley that had, when he first visited, no name.[12]

Here was Kawakita's problem. The Sikha Valley, as it came to be known, on the southwest slope of Annapurna, was, he concluded, "experiencing an ecological disaster of major proportions."[13] Major population growth had led to greater deforestation to clear land and provide fuel, and greater deforestation had led to greater erosion and lesser crop yields, which led in turn to more deforestation. Kawakita, no longer content to document this problem as an academic, wanted to solve it.

He needed to understanding myriad of facts, opinions, and options. How was he to understand the tremendous amount of data he was gathering, so as to find within it the answer to his problem?

Spatial Arrangements Reveal Meaning

Kawakita, writing about his earliest field work in 1951, reported, "With masses of data spread about on my desk, I had been racking my brains to find some way to integrate them when I suddenly realized that depending on the spatial arrangement of the cards, you can see new meaning in them and find ways to synthesize the data. That was the first realization that led to the creation of the KJ Method."[14]

Kawakita later devised what has since become known worldwide as the KJ method. Scientific methods of the mid twentieth century often attempted to fit data into predetermined general categories. Kawakita instead wanted to "let the facts speak for themselves."[15] He began writing down individual elements of data on cards and sorting those cards to reveal relationships. He would give these clusters of cards a title and so discover a theme. He would link common themes under greater headings. In this way, Kawakita revealed the meaningful relationships inherent in the data and transformed an overwhelming amount of data into a manageable set of insights. Kawakita used this method to identify two simple technological innovations—ropelines for transporting fodder, firewood, and manure and pipelines for bringing clean water to villages—that could dramatically improve the life of the people in these villages while bringing their ecosystem back into balance. He worked tirelessly over the next two decades to implement these innovations.

A Visual Foundation for TQM

Kawakita believed that his KJ method had far broader application and utility. The following year, 1964, he wrote a booklet entitled *Pati gaku,* or *Partyship,* applying the method to business applications. *Pati gaku* became immediately and widely popular in Japanese business and government.[16] Many readers requested further detail, which led to the publication in 1967 of *Hassoho,* or *Abduction,* followed by a training system for the method, *Zoko Hassoho,* or *Abduction: Part 2.*[17] The title, *Abduction,* refers to the theory of American pragmatist Charles S. Pierce, who considered abduction to be "the process of *the formation of the hypothesis,*" and "a *meta-scientific* form of reasoning to be used to sort our chaotic, erroneous, ideas and confusions"[18] at a higher order of cognitive thought than either deduction or induction.

The KJ method became integral to a movement—known in the United States as TQM (total quality management)—that transformed business productivity worldwide, first in Japan in the 1960s and 1970s and then in America in the 1980s. The simplified essence of Kawakita's more extensive KJ method was introduced to the United States as "affinity diagramming," one of seven management and planning tools widely disseminated based on the research and publications of the Union of Japanese Scientists and Engineers.[19]

The essence of the KJ method (also known as affinity diagramming)—the visual aggregation of individual data points to reveal emergent themes otherwise hidden in the data—is a primary influence in the Grounded Visioning process. Every time we post a sticky note, and then another, and then another, and move those together to form a cluster of like ideas, we are practicing a variation of the KJ method invented on the slopes of the Himalayas.

HOW OFFICE ARRANGEMENT RELATES TO STRATEGIC PLANNING

On the other side of the globe, another problem needed to be solved that would one day help us create a Grounded Vision. Two brothers, Wolfgang and Eberhard Schnelle, sold office furniture in Germany in the 1970s.[20] Their problem was that people couldn't place orders for furniture until they first defined their needs and designed their offices. The Schnelle brothers were like house builders who needed to learn architectural design to help their confused clients be ready to build. To sell furniture, the Schnelles needed a set of tools that would help clients define their needs, picture their spaces, and make decisions about them.

From necessity, the brothers turned from office sales to office design and lay-out consulting. In the process they developed an innovative, highly visual set of tools, eventually known as Metaplan. The Metaplan tools were so valuable to clients that, once their offices were designed and populated with furniture, clients asked the brothers to help them solve problems in other areas of their businesses. Soon the brothers left the office furniture business and founded Metaplan, an influential consulting company based in Quickborn, Germany.

Again, Sorting Cards to See the Big Picture

Eberhard Schnelle's 1979 book, *The Metaplan-Method: Communication Tools for Planning and Learning Groups,*[21] details these tools and tells why they work so well. A fundamental tool, known as the "card question" or "card sort" method, is similar to the KJ method's "affinity diagram." Participants individually write ideas on cards, one idea per card, and pass them to a moderator, or "communica-tion butler," as Schnelle would say. The moderator would then pin the cards to freestanding, foam core display boards. He or she would further assist the partic-ipants in grouping the cards in clusters and in assigning these clusters a header. Priorities would be set by multi-voting using adhesive dots.

Schnelle made a number of interesting observations about the power of this method.

For example, in the Schnelle brothers' research to create their planning system, they began to measure an indicator of communication complexity they called "utterances per hour."[22] One person speaking for one hour would yield an aver-age of 1 u.p.h. Sixty persons speaking in one hour would be an average of 60 u.p.h. They determined that the maximum u.p.h. in a typical meeting was 100. In a difficult meeting on very complex topics, the u.p.h. was closer to 20 or 30. The Schnelles mapped these utterances over a distribution of participants, enabling them to see that in typical meetings, often very few individuals were responsible for most comments.

By encouraging participants to write individual ideas on cards for posting (an idea carried forward into Grounded Visioning), the Schnelles were able to dramatically increase the number of utterances per hour, up to 300 to 600 for a group of 20, while increasing the distribution of comments throughout the group.

Learn More...

Great Overview of the KJ Method (Affinity Diagramming) and Other Visual Quality Tools

The Memory Jogger Plus: Featuring the Seven Management and Planning Tools by Michael Brassard (Salem, NH: GOAL/QPC, 1996).

Graphic, Visual Tools for Strategic Planning, Team Planning, Personal Development, and Customer Research

Visual Planning Systems by Grove Consultants International at www.grove.com (accessed May 28, 2008).

The large group process of Grounded Visioning extends this idea by breaking a large group into many small groups that work simultaneously in parallel. With the Statewide Nonprofit Association described in Chapter 9, for example, 250 people working at more than 30 tables of 8 were able to speak, work, and visualize data simultaneously.

Figure 14.1
Insights from the Vision Wall: When ideas are posted, people easily see connections.

Illustration by Cindy Murphy.

Empirical Benefits of Visual Thinking

Schnelle's Metaplan pioneers observed a number of other benefits from their highly visual methods, which have at their heart the practice of writing things down and posting them:[23]

- Keeps groups from "going around in circles," assuring speakers that their ideas have been heard, and therefore don't need to be repeated.
- Helps to store ideas in a "group memory" so that participants can readily recall important ideas that were contributed earlier.
- Increases the ability of participants to absorb information by presenting it in a visual form, and keeping it in view.
- Prevents misunderstanding by documenting what has been said.
- Enables participants entering late to quickly come up to speed.
- Contributes over time to the development of a shared, common understanding.

The rule of one idea per card offers a number of participation benefits:

- Keeps ideas visible to participants, as opposed to long lists of ideas on flip chart pads which are rapidly hidden from view.
- Allows individual ideas to be moved together in one or more groupings, as opposed to ideas on flip chart pads which are fixed.
- Allows individuals to see their own work and how it fits into the work of the whole.[24]

"Experience shows," concluded Schnelle, "that the eye is a better recipient and transmitter of information to the brain than the ear."[25] "If eyes and ears together have 100% capacity to absorb information, 70% to 80% of this alone is absorbed by the eyes."[26] Participants in Metaplan sessions use not only the standard "voice/ear" communication channel of speaking but also the powerful "hand/eye" channel of writing and posting. Practitioners of Metaplan brought their highly stylized and effective techniques to the United States from Europe about the same time that the KJ method was being disseminated in the United States from Japan.

THE VISUAL ADVANTAGE FOR GROUNDED VISIONING

Thus the core technique, by which Grounded Visioning processes information visually, is derived from these twin influences: the KJ method (the affinity diagram method) and the Metaplan card sort method. Each of these methods use the extraordinary visual capacities of the healthy human brain, including:[27]

- Spatial relation, or "the position of objects in space."
- Visual discrimination, or "the ability to differentiate objects based on their characteristics" (such as color or shape).
- Whole/part relationships, or "the relationship between an object and a symbol in its entirety and the component parts which make it up."

These methods are powerful because they tap our innate intuition and our remarkable visual information processing abilities, to help us see "the forest for the trees."

So, for example, in the Horticultural Society described in Chapter 9, that group of 70 used a huge wall to visualize the outputs of their work groups. The proposed dreams, hopes, and aspirations, first voiced in groups and subsequently posted on the wall for all to see, covered an enormous space, perhaps 30 feet by 10 feet. Many of the individuals in the room entered it dispirited, perhaps even despairing. Yet the slow, methodical, and highly visual process of aggregating what seemed to be isolated notions into a set of emergent themes across this huge wall had a compelling, irresistible quality to it. The data wouldn't lie, and the visual storytelling made it easy to understand and even inescapable. The people in that room still had the passion to reinvent this old, tired organization. By mapping it out on the wall, this became plain for all to see.

NOTES

1. Thomas G. West, *Thinking Like Einstein: Returning to Our Visual Roots with the Emerging Revolution in Computer Information Visualization* (Amherst, NY: Prometheus Books, 2004), 61.

2. Edward R. Tufte, *The Visual Display of Quantitative Information* (Cheshire, CT: Graphics Press, 1983); see www.edwardtufte.com (accessed May 28, 2008).

3. Anna Adam and Helen Mowers, "Get Inside their Heads with Mind Mapping," *School Library Journal* 53, no. 9 (September 2007): 24.

4. "DHS Launches National Center Focusing on Data Visualization," *Journal of Environmental Health* 67, no. 3 (October 2004): 38.

5. http://web.singnet.com.sg/%7Eaxon2000/article.htm (accessed May 28, 2008).

6. http://www.edge.org/documents/archive/edge87.html (accessed May 28, 2008).

7. "Groxis's Visualized Search Goes to the Web," *InformationWeek,* May 10, 2005, http://find.galegroup.com/itx/infomark.do?&contentSet=IAC-Documents&type=retrieve &tabID=T003&prodId=ITOF&docId=A132340770&source=gale&userGroupName=con &version=1.0 (accessed April 17, 2008).

8. Kym Gilhooly, "Business on the Map: Mind-Mapping Tools Make Inroads into Corporate IT as They Streamline Problem-Solving and Help Structure Tasks," *Computerworld* 40, no. 27 (July 3, 2006): 26.

9. http://www.buzanworld.com/ (accessed May 28, 2008).

10. Thomas G. West, *In the Mind's Eye: Visual Thinkers, Gifted People with Dyslexia and Other Learning Difficulties, Computer Images, and the Ironies of Creativity* (Amherst, NY: Prometheus Books, 1997), 11.

11. West, *Thinking Like Einstein,* 61.

12. http://www.rmaf.org.ph/Awardees/Biography/BiographyKawakitaJir.htm (accessed May 28, 2008).

13. Ibid.

14. Jiro Kawakita, *The Original KJ Method,* rev. ed. (Meguro: Kawakita Research Institute, 1991), 25.

15. http://www.rmaf.org.ph/Awardees/Biography/BiographyKawakitaJir.htm (accessed May 28, 2008).

16. Shoji Shiba and David Walden, *Four Practical Revolutions in Management: Systems for Creating Unique Organizational Capability* (Portland, OR: Productivity Press, 2001), 218.

17. Raymond Scupin, "The KJ Method: A Technique for Analyzing Data Derived from Japanese Ethnology," *Human Organization* 56, no. 2 (1997): 234.

18. Ibid.

19. Shiba and Walden, *Four Practical Revolutions in Management,* 218.

20. http://www.12manage.com/methods_schnelle_metaplan.html (accessed May 28, 2008).

21. Eberhard Schnelle, *The Metaplan-Method: Communication Tools for Planning and Learning Groups,* Metaplan Series No. 7 (Hamburg: Quickborn, 1979).

22. Ibid., 11.

23. Ibid., 12.

24. Neill McKee, Maruja Solas, and Hermann Tillmann, eds., *Games and Exercises* (New York: Communication Section, UNICEF-ESARO and Organizational Learning and Development Section, UNICEF-New York, 1998), 4.

25. Schnelle, *The Metaplan-Method,* 12.

26. Ibid., 18.

27. http://www.incrediblehorizons.com/visual-processing.htm (accessed May 28, 2008).

PART IV

Grounded Visioning in the
Living Organization

15

Case Studies: Business Planning

Grounded Visioning is a way to gain market knowledge and tap employee insights.

Some men see things as they are and ask, "Why?" I dream things that never were and ask, "Why not?"

—George Bernard Shaw

One of the best ways I have found to learn new group processes is by watching a talented leader implement them with an actual organization in a real situation. I have sat at the back, rapidly taking notes, transfixed by the masterful application of general principles to a very specific and unique situation. I may not be able to provide that experience for you as a reader, but I would like to give you the next best thing.

That's why I will share applications of the Grounded Visioning methodology in a variety of actual organizational settings. You can see the methodology tested, stretched, adapted, and integrated in numerous diverse ways. You'll hear what the team wanted, what they needed, and what they got. By reading these cases, you will get a better sense of where to stretch the methodology and where to keep it tight. You will hear how real people responded to the exercises I have described and what results they produced. And most of all you will see how transformative this experience can be, in the very brief time frames I have promised.

GROUNDED VISIONING CAN SPARK LONG-TERM COMPETITIVENESS

In this chapter, I consider planning in the context of the for-profit business. The classic business plan[1] reveals the fundamental planning concerns of business: vision, market analysis, competitive analysis, strategy, products, marketing, operations, and finance. My concern here is primarily with vision: both as a by-product of the dictates of the other seven areas and as a driver of action in those areas.

The key planning challenge in business, especially fast-growth businesses, is focus:

- There are typically many opportunities, too many to pursue. Which to choose?
- There are typically many threats, too many to neutralize. Which to worry most about?
- There are typically never enough resources to do everything. How to allocate them?

Another planning challenge in business is balance. A business that just focuses on tactics can get blindsided by bigger forces that it never sees coming. A business that just focuses on the big picture can get killed by poor execution. A business that focuses just on operations can lose the rudder of its vision and connection with the customer. A business that just focuses on vision can stumble badly on its operational path. What is needed is a balance of vision and operations and a focus on near-term action guided by a long-term vision.

In this chapter, I examine two cases where a haziness of vision was a key concern and, as always, time was short. The first case features a small construction company undergoing a transition of leadership and business focus. A founder, after 25 years at the helm of a successful remodeling company, sought to foster employee management through a daylong, whole-company visioning session as a prelude to employee ownership and an eventual leadership transition. The founder sought to engage his employees in articulating a vision that would inspire them in moving forward, eventually without him. This company also needed a set of small business planning tools to help align its vision with its operations. Our vision work was framed within that additional requirement.

Consider as you read this case how this small business, with very little time for planning, balances an idealistic conversation about long-term vision with a pragmatic focus on short-term action.

Grounded Visioning Gets Results

Organization: Master Builders
Planning need: Transition to employee ownership
Result: All workers helped create a vision that gives the company a competitive advantage

Organization: Fair Trade Worker-Owned Cooperative
Planning need: Identify long-term goals in the aftermath of strategic success
Result: Broad understanding of and commitment to 20-year goals

The second case features a multi-million-dollar worker-owned cooperative, in the business of selling fair trade coffee and related products, that was seeking to revitalize its long-term vision. In this case, its planning systems were fully functional, so we just focused on the vision.

The task was humbling. Twenty-five years earlier, this same organization had set its vision as the introduction of the then-new concept of fair trade to the American market mainstream. Now, more than two decades later, the group had realized this very "big, hairy, audacious goal."[2] Starbucks and the nation's other largest coffee retailers had begun to align themselves with this small company's vision of how the coffee trade should work. The prospect of creating a new vision for this business hardly felt like an academic exercise, but rather a process of refocusing an intensely creative, transformative power.

As you read this case, notice how this business engages its complete work force, including remote workers, in playful conversations about the future and how it synthesizes the results of those conversations so responsively that the workers eventually embrace the final vision with ease and enthusiasm.

In each short case, my aim is to share what was at stake going in, what actually happened, and what changed as a result. Along the way, I hope to convey some of the trepidation people felt as they committed to a process they didn't entirely understand, what their actual experience was like, and what a difference it made to them as seen with the perspective of time. As a consultant, I am very aware of the privilege I enjoy in working so intimately with people and organizations hovering at their growing edge. I share these cases with great respect for their courage and tenacity.

MASTER BUILDERS FACES THE TRANSITION TO EMPLOYEE OWNERSHIP

Many companies come to consultants because they are struggling and need to get back on track. A fortunate few come because they are thriving and want to stay on track. The high-end design/build remodeling company that we'll call Master Builders was in the latter situation.

Founded in the early 1980s by the then and current owner, the company grew slowly, building its reputation on twin commitments to make easy, friendly relations with its clients and to always field a talented, diverse crew. In the last decade, it began offering design/build services. Within two years, it was both designing and building 90 percent of its projects. Most of its jobs are improvement projects in single-family homes, typically including the standard array of kitchen and bathroom renovations, attic and basement conversions, additions, decks and porches, and whole-house renovations.

Recently Master Builders won the Guildmaster Award, presented to building service companies for outstanding quality and customer service. One of the requirements is that 90 percent of the company's customers must be willing to recommend the service to a friend in a project completion survey. Said the owner, "I think our clients appreciate that our accountability holds over time. We have a very well developed program of revisiting past jobs at regular intervals to see if anything needs fixing or touching up. It helps us know what works over time and what doesn't. It's part of our process of continuous improvement."

After more than a quarter century of building and running his own business, the founder and owner realized he was overdue to map a succession strategy. Inspired by John Abrams, cofounder and CEO of South Mountain Company, a 30-year-old employee-owned design and building company on Martha's Vineyard, Massachusetts, and author of *The Company We Keep*,[3] he decided to move toward greater employee management as a step toward an eventual goal of employee ownership. Longtime employees were startled. They were comfortable with the owner making the sales and setting the bar. They were anxious about the added responsibility required by employee management, let alone employee ownership. A few left in search of a more traditional construction company hierarchy. The owner persisted, and those that stayed, along with recent hires, remained cautiously optimistic about the new approach.

How to Connect Vision to a Strategic Plan

At this point, the owner approached me about leading a visioning exercise to engage the whole company in creating its future. A personnel committee, acting also as a *de facto* employee management team, met with me and the owner to review the approach. Working with a group of carpenters poses its own set of challenges. By and large, they tend to be a pragmatic, physical bunch. They have little patience for abstraction and yet are intensely loyal to anything that works reliably. They don't like to sit still for long periods of time, yet really enjoy the camaraderie of groups. The challenge was to present them with a planning process that they could experience as immediately useful in a concrete, tangible way. A central element would be a Grounded Visioning session that, with its focus on stories and its highly visual nature, could be engaging to this very demanding audience.

I was given a precious day to work with the whole company. A Grounded Visioning experience would take about half that time. Additional conversations about values and ideal clients and projects would take the rest. As I often do with small, fast-growth companies, I employed a simple yet powerful planning template developed by Verne Harnish called the "one-page strategic plan" to serve as a straightforward planning framework.[4] The premise behind the one-page strategic plan is that fast-growth companies are all about focus. They have to be. It's the difference between driving 120 miles per hour and 60 miles per hour. You don't have the same margin for error and even small choices matter. The idea is that if you can't condense your business plan to a single page (okay, it is really two pages, but it's still one page, back to back), then you don't really know what you are doing.

I start with the editable version that is freely available to anyone from the downloads section of www.gazelles.com.[5] Then I customize it for the individual business, adding key indicators. With elegant simplicity, the one-page strategic plan moves from the big picture all the way to what you do on Monday morning.

To complete it, you must ask yourself several fundamental questions about your business. Answering these questions takes thoughtful discussion. These discussions would form the basis for the series of conversations planned for our day.

How Does Master Builders Act upon Its Values?

The one-page strategic plan starts with purpose and values. Master Builders was already blessed with a well-articulated set of core values, so we didn't need to surface these for the first time through appreciative stories. Instead, we used the values as a screen to seek out and surface stories of these very values in action, being lived in the day-to-day decisions of the workers. We solicited stories of these values in being put into practice:

- We plan ahead.
- We keep in touch. (We call them before they have to call us.)
- We always wipe our feet. (We show respect, and we expect respect.)
- We care about our work today and tomorrow. (We do it right.)
- We give as good as we get.
- We follow up.
- We say "no" early enough. (We admit to ourselves what we just can't or won't do.)
- We work with someone's nature rather than fight it.
- We attack one problem at a time.

With the values in place, and grounded with stories, we were set to stretch everyone's thinking into the future. The one-page strategic plan asks companies to articulate what Jim Collins calls a "Big Hairy Audacious Goal," or BHAG, achievable over 10 to 20 years.[6] For this challenge we introduced an alternative visioning methodology—"headlines"—as a supplement to our use of appreciative interviews as a spark plug for envisioning the future. I held up a copy of *Remodeling Magazine* and invited folks to imagine their company on the cover in 2020. I asked them to assume that the story was a great one and to work in groups to tell us all the headline and to give us the featured achievements. People threw themselves into this task with great enthusiasm and laughter.

Three themes emerged from the reports from the future:

- **We are the leaders in the green remodeling movement.** We set the standards and the example, measure our impact, and make a measurable performance improvement in our projects. We are a "net zero" company, building homes that consume zero energy.
- **We are renowned for our commitment to good building, fine carpentry, craftsmanship, and attention to traditional details.** People want to work for us, to be part of something exciting. Our projects have a momentum that revitalizes and energizes us.
- **We are making green by being green.** We are a profitable company. We achieve success through employee management and ownership.

Ambitious? Yes. Idealistic? Perhaps, but also potentially very good business. For as Gary Hirshberg, "CE-Yo" of Stonyfield Farm, writes, "A small but growing number of businesses...now realize that reducing carbon pollution can actually be profitable."[7]

Grounded Visioning Yields 10 Aspirations

The one-page strategic planning process asks the company to define measurable success indicators and targets for three- to five-year and one-year time frames. Master Builders wasn't ready to map out a five-year set of metrics yet, but its one-year targets were mostly in place. The company workers quickly confirmed their 12-month targets for revenues, profits, backlog, qualified leads, cash, estimate accuracy, and client satisfaction. New metrics and targets were added for employee satisfaction and green building impact.

With metrics in place, we were set to dive into visioning for the coming year. I set up people in pairs with the appreciative interviewing task, and focused them on the dreams, hopes, and aspirations question. Then one by one, as in all Grounded Visioning sessions, individuals brought their three hopes, written on sticky notes, to the front of the room to declare them and post them for all to see. We used the small group process even though we had 20 people in the room. That's because our design goal was to build a greater sense of individual participation and whole-company perspective.

The visioning process yielded 10 aspirations that clustered into five broad priorities, as follows:

- Efficiency/profitability: Greater efficiency, finish jobs on schedule, broader post-mortem, better information sharing, equipment.
- Education: education, community.
- Green.
- Marketing/community/sales: Marketing and sales.
- Client satisfaction: Design/build as dialogue.

The day came to a close with the participants reorganizing themselves into three work groups to map out implementation steps—quarter by quarter—for the company's top three priorities in the coming year—efficiency/profitability, education, and green. Each group was empowered to make a plan and implement it.

Initially the owner gave these three groups a great deal of autonomy, partly to see would happen: "I felt like we were flailing after the meeting, and that people weren't paying enough attention. But now I get from the company that there is an emerging sense of direction. The guys are saying this has been a really good thing."

The three work groups were in fact moving forward, albeit with fits and starts. The education group laid out an ambitious two-year calendar of skill building in employee management, green remodeling, and fine carpentry technique.

The efficiency/profitability group instituted a new lead carpenters' meeting which met biweekly to assess progress toward metrics. The lead carpenters started gathering their project crews daily for short "huddles," held while standing on the job site, to plan the work day, stress efficiencies, and identify obstacles to be solved. A simple quarterly profit-sharing system was implemented to reward crews directly for meeting the company's project profitability metrics.

New Insights into Energy Consumption, Competitive Power

Perhaps the slowest start, but with the strongest finish, was the green group. This group was initially overwhelmed by the size of the task: "What is a standard for green remodeling that makes us proud, and that we can deliver?" Many firms can remodel and reduce energy consumption by 25 to 40 percent. In this time of global warming crisis, can we remodel by super-insulation and reduce energy consumption by 60 to 80 percent? And then make up the balance by photovoltaic panels or other on-site generation? Can we be the company that routinely delivers a net zero energy house?

"We discovered that nobody is keeping score on energy consumption reduction," said the owner. "Everybody is saying they are green, and leaving it at that. We know how to keep score—through modeling software and measurement tools we use. We can set targets and hit them. That is a tremendous competitive advantage in an area that will soon be an exploding growth opportunity." Within six months the company had its first two super-insulation retrofit projects under contract. Increasingly Master Builders is promoting its capabilities as a green remodeler, with a vision of someday routinely producing net zero homes that produce as much energy as they consume over the course of a year.

FAIR TRADE WORKER-OWNED COOPERATIVE ASKS "WHAT'S NEXT?"

One of the most exciting things about a vision is that it can feel at once both extraordinarily ambitious and also somehow attainable, given time and luck. Jim Collins gave us the term of BHAG—big hairy audacious goals—for visionary ideas that inspire us so.[8] A BHAG is:

- A huge, daunting challenge with a 10- to 30-year time horizon.
- A clear and compelling catalyst for team spirit and unified effort.
- A desired result that reaches out and grabs you, and requires little or no explanation.

In short, these goals are a big stretch, but still within reach if we all work together.

Once a company has actually set such a vision for itself and accomplished it, two things happen right away. It earns the right to set a new vision. And the people in the organization feel both giddy in their accomplishment and humbled by having set such an audacious goal and then achieved it. It makes them think: "Wow, we have a lot of power! What's next?"

20-Year Effort Established Fair Trade in the Marketplace

We were approached by a remarkable fair trade worker-owned cooperative[9] at just such a place. It was founded 20 years earlier by three young men who met once a week for three years trying to conceive a business that would be:

- A social change organization that would help farmers and their families gain more control over their economic futures.
- A group that would educate consumers about trade issues affecting farmers.
- A provider of high-quality foods that would nourish the body and the soul.
- A company that would be controlled by the people who did the actual work.
- A community of dedicated individuals who believed that honesty, respect, and mutual benefit are integral to any worthwhile endeavor.

They settled on "fair trade" as the means by which they would simultaneously build a business, provide a valued service to customers, and compensate their third-world producers, with coffee as their product. Fair trade was a nascent practice in Europe at that time but was virtually unknown in the United States.

Fair trade as they chose to practice it embraced several notions that were then radical in American business:

- Small farmers should not be condemned to live in poverty for their efforts in growing a highly valued product.
- Small farmers should receive a minimum price per pound as a fair share for their labor regardless of the fluctuations of the underlying commodity market.
- Small farmers should receive a premium above the market rate for delivering quality and certified organic products and for practicing ecologically sustainable farming that benefits their community and the planet.
- Small farmers should be organized in cooperatives wherever possible to sell their products directly so that more compensation goes to producers and less to middlemen.

The story of what happened next could fill a book of its own. Let's just say that Mahatma Gandhi, when he said, "First they laugh at you. Then they ridicule you. Then they fight you. Then you win," could have been talking about them. Today there are more than 400 coffee companies purchasing at least a portion of their coffee under Fair Trade terms, including the biggest names in the business. There is a global Fair Trade label and certifying organization. And the little cooperative that could has millions in sales, a large work force, and a full line of fairly traded products.

Finding the Middle Ground between Mission and Quarterly Plans

About this time, the cooperative approached me, having realized its founding vision, with the question, "What's next?"

The company already enjoyed a well-regarded mission that it hoped would guide it for the next 100 years. It already benefited from the rigorous pursuit of a four-year planning process that consistently delivered both growth and success. But the vast middle ground—the space in which a compelling vision might stand as a beacon, toward which their four-year plans could take them, in alignment with their mission—remained unclear.

These good people had already been busy, and they were stuck. They had searched their cooperative networks for ideas and inspiration to help in creating such a vision but had found little. Undaunted, they formed a visioning group of three board members and set off on their own. First they engaged their worker owners in contributing to the process, asking them to envision a newspaper headline 20 years into the future that expressed some kind of success they'd like to see. This is a great technique for releasing oneself from the limits of present-day thinking, while still grounding the future image in something tangible like a newspaper headline.

The workers responded playfully, individually creating dozens of vivid images of their organization enjoying a very positive future. Among them were items like the following:

- "Our Cooperative Adds 500th Member"
- "Fair Trade Leader Launches Coffee Shops in 10 Major Cities"
- "Our Wine Surpasses Gallo in Gallons Sold"

How to Involve Every Worker?

This, after some delay, is where we came in. The visioning group had lots of great data, but no real information. It needed to take its work to the next level and bring it to fruition. Together, we created a "plan to plan," which mapped out the steps by which we'd engage the worker owners in further dialogue about the vision, involve the board in crafting it, and engage the worker owners once again in reviewing, approving, and embracing the final vision. And we designed this plan to make full use of the good work the visioning group had already done, adapting Grounded Visioning to the cooperative's unique needs.

We turned next to the headline data, clustering it into roughly similar content groups expressing related, visionary scenarios. Several, for example, imagined their company as the largest worker cooperative in the country. Others pictured their company as having an enormous economic justice impact. Others saw themselves teaching corporate America a much-needed lesson in doing business ethically.

The visioning group wanted to involve every worker in the company. That meant convening a short, face-to-face meeting for 90 minutes with the East Coast workers. And that meant holding a shorter virtual meeting with the West Coast workers. We presented the East Coast workers with our feedback on their own ideas and used it as our spark plug in lieu of the appreciative interviews. We engaged them in a discussion about which of the various future scenarios seemed most appealing. Then, using adhesive dots, we asked them to multi-vote for their top three. A few favorites clearly emerged.

At this point we gave a quick tutorial on BHAGs[10]—what they are and how they are made. BHAGs typically come in one of four forms. They can be:

- Quantitative: Wal-Mart once aimed to be a 125 billion dollar company by 2000.
- Qualitative: Citibank's aim to be the most powerful, serviceable bank in the world.
- Competitive: Avis's "We try harder" aimed at Hertz.
- Role modeled: Stanford's "Be the Harvard of the west" in the 1940s.

After presenting this concept, we asked the workers to use them in drafting possible BHAGs inspired by the vision scenarios from the headlines. We were asking them to share their dreams, hopes, and aspirations, but in a particular form that would serve their business planning purposes. They did so enthusiastically, posing dreams like the following:

- Our coop has two million loyal consumers who actively choose fair trade.
- Our coop is at the center of the world's largest network of fair trade.
- Our coop models a viable cooperative alternative to globalization.

We then repeated this process for the West Coast workers using a web-based meeting platform. We now had input from every worker owner who wished to participate.

Board Builds on Workers' Ideas

The board members were now ready to do their part. They had all the information they needed from the workers in the company. They just needed to wade into it and find its essence. They had before them:

- The original envisioned headlines in the workers' own words.
- The vision clusters of similar headlines and their ranking by the workers.
- The workers' proposed BHAGs in formats suggested by vision guru Jim Collins.

The board experienced roughly the same process as had the workers—first reacting to the vision scenarios and then doing their own multi-voting.

Next we reviewed Collins's thinking, and then they wrote their own BHAGs. Finally, we posted all the proposed BHAGs, including those of the workers and those just envisioned by the board members. Now we were ready for some great conversation about what the organization really wanted to be and where it wanted to go.

After some very creative and heartfelt give-and-take and another round of multi-voting, a clear consensus vision emerged. The day ended with each board member drafting a few words or phrases picturing how they'd know the vision had come to pass—what Jim Collins calls a "vivid description."

The final vision statement—the company's preferred future described eloquently in just 24 words—was approved by the board at its next meeting:

> There will be...a vibrant mutually cooperative community of two million committed participants trading fairly one billion dollars a year in a way that transforms the world.

A vivid description—a narrative picturing the vision as fulfilled in six concise paragraphs—was approved at the one just after. Board members commented on the immediate, practical implications of the vision and how it would surely shape the next four-year plan. "This work is already affecting the way I think about budgets, and priorities, and strategic partnerships," said one.

Next the visioning group met to craft definitions for pivotal terms used in the vision statement. Group members hoped to clarify for the worker owners—who must ultimately approve the vision—what the board meant by the words used. They also aimed to create a reference for future co-op members in the years to come, who might wonder what precisely did the Board of 2006 have in mind in using these key 24 words? Those definitions were then shared with the broader board for review and approval.

The vision and vivid description then went before the worker owners for their review and approval. The worker owners embraced the vision by a vote of 45 to 2. Some consultants argue that all any business really needs is a 20-year goal and a 90-day plan. Everything else should fall into place.

Action Steps to a 20-Year Vision

This cooperative felt the need for a clear, 20-year vision, and they put it in place by taking these 10 action steps, which any organization could follow:

- Start with your board and engage their commitment to the process.
- Learn more about what vision means by reading Jim Collins's and Jerry Porras's article in *Harvard Business Review*, "Building Your Company's Vision."[11]
- Be clear on why you need a vision and how it fits into your other big ideas, like mission and values, that also guide your business.
- Engage every worker in a process—like the headlines exercise—that inspires their imagination and creativity about their dreams, hopes, and aspirations.
- Work toward common ground through the clustering of related ideas and by multi-voting among priorities.
- Translate your most promising candidates into possible BHAGs, using the Collins/Porras formats, before clustering them and multi-voting among them yet again.
- Know you've found the vision when it is both too wonderful to turn away from and almost too scary to face.
- Make it come alive through vivid description.
- Take whatever time you need to internalize your vision and make it your own.
- Allow the compelling nature of the goal to draw you forward toward making it real.

NOTES

1. http://www.businesstown.com/planning/creating-outline.asp (accessed May 28, 2008).

2. James C. Collins and Jerry I. Porras, "Building Your Company's Vision," *Harvard Business Review* 74, no. 5 (September–October 1996): 65.

3. John Abrams, *The Company We Keep—Reinventing Small Business for People, Community, and Place* (White River Junction, VT: Chelsea Green Publishing Company, 2005).

4. Verne Harnish, *Mastering the Rockefeller Habits: What You Must Do to Increase the Value of Your Growing Firm* (New York, NY: Select Books, 2002).

5. www.gazelles.com (accessed May 28, 2008).

6. Collins and Porras, "Building Your Company's Vision," 65.

7. Gary Hirshberg, *Stirring It Up—How to Make Money and Save the World* (New York: Hyperion, 2008), 84.

8. Collins and Porras, "Building Your Company's Vision," 65.

9. Portions of this case are based on my previously published work, which may be found at http://www.ourbiz.biz/2006/11/index.html.

10. Collins and Porras, "Building Your Company's Vision," 65.

11. Ibid.

16

Case Studies: Nonprofit Planning

Grounded Visioning engages the passion and commitment of volunteers.

I am because we are.

—African proverb

This chapter considers planning in the context of the nonprofit organization. The nonprofit organization holds as paramount its pursuit of mission, not profit. The federal government grants this sector a privileged tax-free status to encourage the investment of talent and money, guided by voluntary boards, into areas of society that would otherwise be neglected in a purely capitalist economy. Visioning in the nonprofit sector is unique and can be quite challenging: the shared vision must directly address society's most intractable problems, while simultaneously being compelling enough to draw donor investment and attractive enough to draw volunteer labor and stewardship.

The nonprofit sector is sometimes called the voluntary sector because its leadership—through its boards—is composed of volunteers. And many of its workers are volunteers—think "unpaid staff"—as well, though typically guided by paid professionals. So the "currency," if you will, in nonprofit planning is passion. People must care enough about the work of the organization to take time and money away from their businesses and their families and give it instead to their organization of choice. Planning is an extraordinary opportunity to engage the passions of volunteers, so as to win their commitment of work, wisdom, and wealth.

It has become fashionable in recent years in business to talk about the "double bottom line," referring first of course to the organization's net profit but second to its net positive impact on society. Nonprofit organizations have historically and routinely juggled the demands of both these bottom lines, although they typically put the net positive impact on society first. They focus on the second bottom line—what they call creating a positive fund balance—only to enable them to live another day to contribute to society.

Many nonprofit organizations find themselves focusing on two major areas in planning: impact and infrastructure. Impact means all the ways in which they improve the lives of what Peter Drucker calls their "primary customer."[1] Visioning among nonprofits often means imagining how the world will be better for those the organization serves, be they individuals, communities, or the environment. This defines the "ends," and it is critical to stoking the passion that keeps people working and contributing within the nonprofit sector.

Infrastructure means all the ways in which organizations must develop themselves in order to be effective in serving the primary customer. Typically this includes concerns such as facilities, resource development, marketing, staff development, and board development, among others. Visioning among nonprofits thus also means imagining how the organization can be the best that it can be at doing what it does. This defines the "means" and is critical to keeping the organization competitive and effective.

TWO VERY DIFFERENT CASES SHOW HOW VISION INSPIRES COMMITMENT

In the first case, we consider a challenge from the world of health care: a hospital that also functions as a center of higher education. Health care and higher education are two of the largest, most sophisticated, and most well-endowed segments of the nonprofit sector. Therefore, the challenges of managing a large hospital or university can be far more complex than that of managing a small business.

Nevertheless, in this case some of the core themes of nonprofit planning find expression. The Medical Center Division must concern itself first and foremost with its impact on its primary customers—its patients. Yet it must also feed the passions of its teaching staff and medical students to keep their interest and engagement high. It must balance the need to serve its patients and retain its staff and students with the need to meet the funding priorities of large agencies and foundations that sustain its growth and innovation.

Grounded Visioning Gets Results

Organization: University Medical Center Division
Planning need: Transition to new leadership, build collaboration among different disciplines
Result: New credibility for the whole division and a leadership role in patient-centered health care

Organization: Urban Pilot Public High School
Planning need: With limited time, create strategic plan and energize volunteers
Result: New commitment to college preparedness, successful fund-raising

---

In the second case, we consider an urban public high school that serves as a pilot for innovation in a large urban public school system. Being an innovator in a large urban public school system can be a difficult, thankless task. To be free to innovate, many pilot schools fight to gain autonomy from the sometimes burdensome or bureaucratic regulations and practices common in large systems. In exchange for this, they often give up access to a larger pool of financial and capacity building resources also common in large systems. So they may find themselves richer in autonomy yet poorer in resources.

They must be creative in tapping the passions of those in their community to help them succeed. Yet urban public school communities typically lack the deep pockets of those gathered around innovative private schools. So they must be especially effective—and creative—in building partnerships and in tapping the time and talents of their community network.

This high school made what for it was a scary choice to bring its entire community together at several large meetings to chart its future. That meant bringing together for planning under a "big tent" a whole host of people who didn't work at the school. This leap of faith to include a wide spectrum of potentially ungovernable community allies, and thereby trust in their best intentions, is one of many inspiring acts that you tend to find among strong nonprofit managers.

UNIVERSITY MEDICAL CENTER DIVISION NAVIGATES THROUGH SKEPTICISM AND LEADERSHIP TRANSITION

A rapidly growing, sprawling division of a distinguished University Medical Center was going through a leadership transition. The division had acquired a recent history of being the center's doormat, taking whatever projects didn't fit elsewhere. The doctors, with their interests in patient-centered and alternative care, were derided as the touchy-feely misfits of the center. For years, many had not only not been rewarded for their work but had also been subjected to ridicule.

The CEO was seeking a new chief of general medicine, geriatrics, and palliative care who would give the division some shape and instill in it some pride. Bypassing tradition, he dug down deep into the ranks, bypassing long-serving men with equally long curriculum vitae, to hire a younger, less proven, woman doctor with a facilitative leadership style and a history of building teams and consensus in her area. He expressed great confidence in her ability, almost more than she had in herself, she would later say, as he offered her the job. She thought hard, talked it over with her family, and took it.

"The division was at a crossroads," she would later reflect. "It had been through a difficult transition, and many of its members had retreated into a virtual cave just to survive. These were highly respected academics, but they had just been pummeled for their views. The division was crawling out from under a rock, and openly questioning, 'What did we have to offer?' Its very worth and identity were in question."

Needed: A Vision Encompassing Clinical Care, Education, Research

She knew that her first step as leader had to be to bring everyone together in the same room, for the first time in the history of the division, to talk about mission and priorities. She imagined that some who wanted her job might want her to fail. She guessed that some who hoped she would succeed would be skeptical of her chances. She knew that doctors had a reputation for having big egos and huge needs for autonomy, but that somehow, if they were all to succeed together, they would have to all work well together. She knew she would have one shot to win them over, and that was it. Her fate would likely be sealed. It was a high risk, high reward strategy, but she felt she had no choice. That is when we were invited to help.

Later she would muse,

> I had no hope of being anything other than what I was as a leader. I wasn't even close enough to the standard that I felt tempted to pretend. I had to go along with my weird self, and be true to that. Had I been closer to the norm, I would have tried harder to blend in, but that wasn't an option. I wanted this retreat to help me get more clear on my own leadership capabilities and style, to overcome the shock of being chosen, and to integrate this role into my own life, and the life of the division. I wanted to see what I had to offer, as a leader, and where I had to grow.

The division retreat was scheduled for an evening and day, seemingly a leisurely pace by Grounded Visioning standards. The appreciative interviews that so often serve as the "spark plugs" for visioning would, in this case, double as a community building exercise, and be extended and combined with dinner, thus functioning as a social activity the evening before the "real work" began. The diverse division, composed of three distinct domains of activity—clinical care, education, and research—would in essence require three distinct visioning sessions, one right after the other, extending throughout the full day.

Physicians with Different Areas of Emphasis Find Common Ground

That first evening the doctors gathered, and the appreciative interviews began to work their magic, charming the participants with their uniquely positive and pleasing perspective on organizational life. Participants shared what attracted them to this organization, including the chance to fundamentally change the system of care, the ability to make a difference, the opportunity to care for under-served populations, a nice group of people with shared interests to work with, and the ability to work with mentors, among others.

Next, the doctors told high point stories of working hard in the clinic, but in a satisfying way; of sitting with residents and watching them experience that flash of "ah ha!" insight; and of getting lost in the moment, serving patients, doing those little things 20 times a day where nothing is missing and everything is complete. After hearing these stories, and more, the doctors were able to affirm that when they are at their very best, they:

- Feel inspired and inspire others.
- Enjoy diverse and satisfying relationships with residents, colleagues, and patients.
- Make a difference.
- Feel valued and create a culture of valuing others.
- Change the way medicine is practiced in fundamental ways.
- Appreciate the moment.
- Overcome barriers and adversity.
- Value balance and quality of life.

Perhaps that night the doctors left pleasantly surprised, intrigued that they had discovered a vivid and satisfying common ground shared with each other. In any event they appeared ready to work the next day. I sent them to assigned seats at round tables, each seating eight, thus ensuring a diversity of clinical disciplines at each table. The day's work would be three rounds of visioning in each of their three, core cross-functional areas of contribution—clinical care, education, and research. Never before had they held conversations about these areas with all disciplines represented at the same time. Historically they would have pursued these topics independently, each within their disciplinary silos, without any benefit of collaboration or synergy.

Table 16.1 shows the agenda for each of the three rounds.

About five priorities emerged in each of the three areas:

- **Clinical care priorities.** Improve systems of care and information, meet unmet needs by expanding access and service, improve coordination of care, improve care experience, improve patient education.
- **Education priorities.** Curriculum development coordination and evaluation, self-reflective learning/wisdom, funding, innovation in education process, institutional change, faculty development, patient and community education.
- **Research priorities.** Create research infrastructure, provide protected time, create research agenda of priority topics, foster collaboration, encourage business.

A variety of current and proposed initiatives were identified for most priorities.

No doubt many of the doctors were dazzled and proud of the diversity of projects planned or underway. The work session ended with an opportunity for all

Table 16.1
Medical Division Grounded Visioning: Agenda

Time (minutes)	Task
10	Explain self-management roles for table work groups, explain task
30	Work in table work groups to brainstorm priorities and select three to five
35	• Present, post, and sort output at table work groups • Set priorities by multi-voting • For top priorities, share related initiatives, current or proposed

participants to make recommendations in the areas of divisional organizational structure, follow-up implementation strategies, and action steps. Three cross-functional work groups—one in each of the key domains—were formed with volunteers to oversee ongoing implementation.

Grounded Visioning Establishes an Identity

Four years later, the chief reflected on the impact of the visioning session:

We didn't know it at the time, and we had a hard time accepting it, and letting it shine, but we were beginning to define ourselves as being different, and wanting to embrace that. In the world of tough medicine and hard science, the soft side is not necessarily something you trot out as an advantage, either personally or as a division. The retreat helped us appreciate ourselves, and gave us a collective sense of who we were. It gave us meaning, on our own terms, and that gave us the strength to go on, even though we were the lowest paid and the least rewarded in the institution. Still we knew who we were, and after that retreat we could proudly identify that to ourselves and to others. Over the past four years we've become increasingly more visible and active leaders in bringing the whole medical school over to that side of medicine. It came as a surprise initially when other people expressed an interest in that. It came as an even bigger surprise when they ultimately rewarded and recognized us for who we were.

Within the Division we have been leading a process of appreciative inquiry for the whole medical center and the whole medical school. Nationally we have become consultants to other medical schools. There is a great hunger there. Most medical schools are under siege, and they are aching for some way to open up their potential. Now we get lots of requests. It has all grown out of the sense that we no longer need to do this on the side, by ourselves. Five years ago we would share what we do under our breath, just waiting for folks to roll their eyes. They thought it was hocus-pocus. Yet now we know that medicine desperately needs right-brained skills: mindfulness, the healers' art, the efficacy of alternative therapies, patient-centered health care, appreciative inquiry—all merged with good research methodology. We have come to represent the right brain of our institution. Some of the most skeptical have become actively curious, and then even integrated some of our practices into their own areas.

The coin of the realm in our world is grants. We just received a million dollar grant to study the development of wisdom in people's response to suffering. A million dollars makes people take notice. They become curious in spite of themselves. This grant has given people in this division a certain kind of legitimacy that others can't ignore. We had 30 faculty four years ago. Now we have 45. We have just added a whole new clinical program and should add 5 to 10 more soon.

From Community, Many Benefits Flow

The chief continued:

What I am discovering when I reflect on the retreat is that it is not so much the concrete things that came out of it that I value, but more the commitment to be a community that works together in a certain way. For example we embraced the concept of cross-disciplinary task forces. Some projects worked, and some did not. But the task force concept worked quite well. That led to joint research proposals, and cross-training of doctors in palliative care to boost capacity across the division. We now operate a collaborative schedule, which gives more people more time off from call. We have been discovering how to use our size and diversity as an advantage.

We are more of an emergent community now. I was not comfortable with that at first. Once we started to define ourselves in terms of who we were as a community, once we started working together in a certain way, things started emerging, some I couldn't predict. I wanted to increase funding, but I had no idea it would be a wisdom grant. I wanted a national reputation, but had no idea it would be for mindfulness and appreciative inquiry. I had to get comfortable with the idea that I could not control and predict everything. It is like being on a river, you just keep paddling and go with the flow.

If there is anything I would say to myself of four years ago, it is to recognize that things take longer that you think. I was so impatient for change, that if something didn't change in a year, I felt it was a failure. I actually felt discouraged after the first year or two, as things were slowly moving along, with no great "ah has!" It's like a flower that grows out of the ground, growing, growing, growing, you think it will never pop, and then one day there it is! It just takes time. Maybe others can do it faster than us, but now, after these years of slowly moving along, we are popping!

We just finished our faculty reviews. One of our faculty shared with me, "So many of my colleagues elsewhere are saying how dismayed they are, and how disillusioned they are with their jobs and situations. I love my colleagues, and I love my work. I feel like I am supported. Yes I am too busy and the system is difficult sometimes, but I feel so positive about where and with whom I work. I am very grateful."

Of course not everyone feels that way, but enough of a core of us does to keep us going. A nucleus within our division feels that they are really making a difference in how medicine is practiced. That gives us the strength to keep going. We hit problems, and we do what we can to overcome them, with care, compassion, and love. I am so grateful. In a very difficult world, things are good.

URBAN PILOT PUBLIC HIGH SCHOOL INVITES ENTIRE COMMUNITY TO CREATE A VISION

Urban High was founded in 1983 as a last resort for disadvantaged or disaffected kids who were failing at a large high school in the city's public system. A staff of six worked with 90 at-risk young people in three grades in an alternative program that operated by a different set of rules. The program valued personal relationships between teachers and students; integrated, flexible curriculum; on-site, shaped decision-making; and learning partnerships with outside organizations. The experiment worked, and the following year the school doubled in size, to 12 faculty, two administrators, and 180 students.

Now, 25 years later, Urban High serves 288 students with 22 teachers and 14 staff member. It is still a pilot school within the larger public school system. There are no academic entrance requirements, and many entering students test below grade level. The student body mirrors that of the larger city: 46 percent African-American, 36 percent Hispanic, 15 percent white, and 3 percent Asian. Year after year, 96 percent of its students graduate, and 94 percent go on to college. Urban High is an award-winning, national model for urban high schools.

An Enviable Graduation Rate

In the last 10 years, Urban High joined the Coalition of Essential Schools, a national network of schools committed to a style that embraces:

- Learning demonstrated by competence, rather than just by grades, arising out of personal relationships with faculty.
- Learning activated by working with core questions and themes, rather than with disconnected subjects, using inquiring "habits of mind."
- Learning by active engagement with the real, adult world of work, in concert with community partner institutions.

The high school's mission, in keeping with this pedagogy, is to "create a socially committed and morally responsible community of learners, which values its students as individuals. Its goal is to encourage academic excellence and the Habits of Mind, self-esteem and leadership development among all the school's students."

Urban High became the kind of school that would inspire a parent to say: "This is one of the most successful models of an urban public school, and also one of the highest performing schools in this city. I have personally witnessed the transformative ability of the school to take America's forgotten youth and turn them into confident, successful individuals who are not just productive members of society but feel a duty to give back."

The school's board had recently hired a new head of school who brought in fresh energy and new ideas. Its strategic plan was obsolete and needed updating. The board, in concert with the new head of school, set out to create a new strategic plan. The process had to fit the inclusive, inquiring culture of the school. It had to make room for the participation of students, parents, community partners, and others with a stake in the future of the school. As much as they all wanted to be included, their time was very limited. The process had to be participatory and powerful but also time-efficient. This is when I was invited to help.

Taking a Risk on Nontraditional Planning

The school's strategic planning committee, working with the consultants, developed a "table of contents" for the final plan and a "plan to plan" mapping out the outcomes and associated tasks for the entire planning process. The committee began its deliberations with traditional ideas about engaging stakeholders through questionnaires, interviews, and stakeholders. Once it understood that it might be possible to bring all the stakeholders together into the same room at the same time to create the plan collaboratively, in a visible expression of community, the committee became intrigued with the idea of using a large group methodology for planning. Committee members marveled at how fast, inclusive, and transparent it could be.

Still, "making the choice to do planning this way was taking a risk," reflected the head of school. "There were people that felt that this is not the traditional way of doing this. They had all sorts of questions. They would say, 'It feels good, but will it give us a strong enough direction?' It was a difficult choice."

The committee eventually made its choice, and decided that every constituency with a stake in the future of the institution would be invited: faculty, staff, administrators, parents, students, alumni, board members, neighbors, educational colleagues, community partners, and business supporters. A list of 100 participants was easy to imagine. Yet it was hard to imagine bringing this group of busy people together more than three times, for three hours each. These few hours became the heart of the planning process, and a simple design emerged featuring three core planning tasks:

- **Assessment.** What are the school's current strengths and weaknesses, and what are the environment's opportunities and threats?
- **Visioning.** What is it that this community most wants to create?
- **Strategies.** How can this community realize its vision?

The heart and soul of the process would be a three-hour Grounded Visioning exercise, sandwiched between an assessment and an implementation exercise.

Step One: Help the Community Understand the School's Current Situation

The three sessions would be held during the late afternoon and evening, when parents and working people would be able to attend. They would be scheduled about two months apart, to minimize the impact of the required time commitment and to allow for some reflection between sessions. They would begin with a light dinner at 4 p.m., food always being a draw, and end no later than 7, when people would likely be ready to go home. The diverse participants would be seated at round tables of eight, with assigned seating to ensure their diversity. One of the school's community partners donated a large meeting room. The design was set, and the invitations went out. So many people were involved, in such an inclusive way, that the organizers took to calling these meetings the "Big Tent" gatherings.

Table 16.2 shows how we structured the agenda for the first "Big Tent" session on assessment.

We invited diverse work groups at each table to brainstorm ideas in each of the four assessment categories and to pick their top three, which they could then report in crisp, two-minute reports. Based on what they had just done, and what they had just heard, we invited them to brainstorm possible goals for the school, and to pick their top three, which they reported in a final, one-minute report.

Table 16.2
High School's Big Tent Meeting on Assessment: Agenda

Time (minutes)	Task
25	Welcome and opening
65	Assess current situation at table work groups:
	• School strengths/weaknesses
	• Environmental opportunities/threats
30	Work group reporters share reports with the whole group
35	Propose possible goals based on assessment, working at tables
15	Work group reporters share quick reports
10	Closing

With this activity we rapidly immersed the community into a deeper understanding of the school's current situation and enabled it to reflect prudently on what that might mean for the future. A summary report of the evening recounted the top ideas in each assessment category and an initial set of possible school goals as they emerged from the final activity.

Step Two: Describe the School at Its Best

The second evening had as its desired outcomes those that Grounded Visioning delivers so quickly:

- Share how the school is when it is at its best.
- Identify beliefs about how we are when we are at our best.
- Share dreams, hopes, and aspirations for the school's future.
- Prioritize dreams, hopes, and aspirations for the school's future.
- Create action plan for next steps.

If the school had had even less time for planning than it did, it could have held only this one session and created the core of a remarkable plan.

Table 16.3 shows how we structured the second evening on visioning.

We invited individuals to share their high point stories at their tables one at a time, and then for each table as a whole to identify common themes. Reporters from each table then were able to quickly report the work group's conclusion to the statement: "When we are at our best, we..." Some groups reported, among others, that we:

- Work and laugh together.
- Think critically.
- Show respect toward each other.
- Practice our core values by taking care of each other.
- Conduct self-evaluation for future growth and improvement.
- Work together toward a common goal.
- Are deliberate in building community and relationships.

Table 16.3
High School Visioning: Agenda

Time (minutes)	Task
15	Welcome and opening
60	Share high point stories in small groups
	• Identify themes and beliefs
	• Work group reporters share one-minute reports
90	Pairs share dreams, hopes, and aspirations
	• Work groups find common themes to put forward as a table
	• Facilitators help merge common themes as tables post and sort
	• Individuals express preferences through multi-voting
15	Closing

Categorize the Vision

The elements of the participants' unfolding vision were expansive and diverse, yet clustered together in seven large areas:

- Expanding and enriching the curriculum
- Improving facilities
- Attaining financial stability
- Expanding partnerships
- Staying small and diverse
- Retaining autonomy within the larger public school system
- Improving communications internally and externally

One hundred participants had created community, identified best practices, and articulated a shared vision in less than three hours. A report of the evening's work summarized the best practices, and recounted every proposed goal, and how they fit together into the seven emergent goal themes. Upon reflection, the planning committee unbundled two of the larger goals (curriculum into core curriculum and electives; communication into internal communication and external outreach) into four, creating a total of nine.

Step Three: Set Strategies to Realize the Vision

The third and final evening focused on strategies to realize this vision. Participants had been given an opportunity to express their preferences as to which of the nine areas they would most like to discuss in greater depth. They were then assigned in advance to a table with others sharing the same interest. These groups were then given almost the entire evening to work together in focused discussion of their area using a discussion template as a guide—asking them to define why the goal is important, assess how the school is performing currently, brainstorm possible strategies to achieve success, pick the top three to five, propose action steps for implementing those top strategies, prepare a report. Reporters had three minutes for these longer reports.

Two years later, the head of school reported,

> We are doing well in terms of the goals set in the strategic planning process. The school is in a good place. In that first year, with faculty, we had to be persistent, engaging them in dialogue about what these goals really meant, and what support I was willing to give to achieve them. There were questions, and disagreements, and we just needed to be clear with everyone, and keep communication open, and stay focused on a positive direction. We stayed true to it, and now everyone realizes we are making a tremendous amount of progress, and it is very gratifying.

Result: New Focus on College Readiness

The head of school continued:

> What emerged was a strong ongoing commitment to curriculum review, which is continuing and on track. A new focus on electives and travel also emerged. Electives have been introduced into the sophomore class, and are going strong this year, and have settled into routine. That first year a group went to the Dominican Republic, and next year a group is going to Brazil.
>
> The biggest innovation has been in the area of college readiness. First we gained a part-time person with the support of a community partner, to help us coordinate our efforts in this area and help students consider a wider range of schools, access more financial aid, gain more parent and teacher support, and build stronger relationships with colleges. Next our development team initiated a capital campaign to endow a permanent, full-time position, and we are half way there. This will mean more students going to better colleges with more aid.
>
> The biggest "pro" from the planning process is how it brought in the voices of a wide number of constituents, and created ownership on the part of many who felt they had played a role in creating it. In fact, one of board members—a parent—chose not to leave the board even though his child had graduated, "because we're not finished in accomplishing these goals, and I intend to stay until they are done." Parents still refer to it, students are still involved because of it, and the faculty knows they were at the table when the goals were set. It might not be a great process for everyone, but we believe in community, and it forced us to say, "Just how much do we really believe in it?"

NOTE

1. Peter F. Drucker, *The Drucker Foundation Self-Assessment Tool—Participant Workbook,* rev. ed. (San Francisco: Jossey-Bass, 1999), 9.

17

Case Studies: Community Planning

When groups are large, diverse, and unwieldy, Grounded Visioning creates focus.

Democracy is a small hard core of common agreement, surrounded by a rich variety of individual differences.

—James B. Conant

I n this chapter, we consider planning in the context of whole communities. In communities there is usually neither the potent organizing principle of the profit motivation nor the shared overarching mission of the nonprofit world. Instead there are patchworks of diverse stakeholders, all with different needs and potentially different priorities, who often pledge no more than to coexist by virtue of living in a democratic society. In these contexts, the need for a collaborative visioning process, in which people discover their common ground together, is even more important.

We have seen that in businesses we can comfortably limit our conversations about vision to our employees, or perhaps expand them to include customers and suppliers. In nonprofit organizations, we can limit ourselves to employees plus our volunteer board members, although we may expand them to include clients, community members, and affected business leaders. In every case, there is a set of relationships and agreements that draws individuals together and gives them common bonds.

In communities our discussions of vision are wide open to any resident that is interested. Organizers of such conversations don't often know who will show up and what they will say. The boundaries of such conversations are far more porous.

People who call themselves residents of the same town may share values, or they may not. The potential for discord and controversy is very great. The community planning process brings these people together, and they come as they are. Many have been conditioned to see community meetings as public hearings, where they are entitled to say their piece as emphatically as they wish, leaving the resolution of divergent views to someone else to worry about. For these citizens to be asked to take responsibility for their views and to harmonize them with that of their neighbors sometimes represents a new—and even startling—behavior. Yet it is a profoundly constructive one, as it leads to that "small hard core of common agreement" that James Conant tells us about.

LARGE, DIVERSE GROUPS CAN COME TOGETHER AROUND GROUNDED VISIONING

Our first case features an old New England town that is gathering input from its citizens for the creation of a comprehensive long-range plan. Residents of New England towns typically cherish a love of autonomy and home rule ("live free or die" being the state motto of New Hampshire, for example), so bringing people together to create shared public priorities can be a lightening rod for controversy.

Note as you read this case how the town uses a series of community gatherings to build consensus for the framing of the critical issues facing the town, without any expert or authority telling the individuals involved what to think or how to behave.

In the second case, a regional community group seeks to put steak with the sizzle of the phrase, "civic engagement," when 400 community members gather to hear their new governor address them on the topic. The organizers don't want to miss this remarkable opportunity to get real work done for real communities. Yet as they face the real challenge of many communities: that the people coming together in the room at the same time are really just strangers, with little obviously in common and much standing in the way of their finding common ground.

Consider as you read this case how the Community Leadership Program charms a group of complete strangers into sharing what they care most about,

---

Grounded Visioning Gets Results

Organization: Our Town
Planning need: Identify priorities at the start of a long-range planning process
Result: Many citizens participate in setting planning committee's agenda

Organization: Community Leadership Program
Planning need: Tap into knowledge and experience of 400 community leaders
Result: New ideas, new initiatives, new connections

in terms of civic engagement, and then engages them in finding common ground and making commitments to take a stand on that ground.

CITIZENS IDENTIFY CHALLENGES TO JUMP START LONG-RANGE PLANNING

New England is graced with many beautiful, historic small towns that have kept much of their integrity in an era of increasing modernization. One town, which we'll just call Our Town, was first home to native American settlements, then a colonial town gathered in 1635, then the birthplace of the American Revolution in 1775, then the birthplace of an American conservation ethic through the writings of Henry David Thoreau and an American transcendental spiritual movement through the writings of Ralph Waldo Emerson in the nineteenth century. More recently, the town has struggled with land use, transportation, economic development, housing, and other challenges common in the twenty-first century.

The board of selectmen and the planning board of the town authorized the formation in 2001 of a comprehensive long-range planning committee with the charge to develop "a comprehensive long range plan for the Town, with goals, objectives, and priorities through the year 2020."[1] In addition to specifying the content areas of the plan, the charge directed the committee to "Plan and conduct an interactive public process to determine community values, goals, and objectives."[2]

Our Town has a history and practice of planning, so the committee members had their hands full just absorbing all the topical studies and plans that had been done since 1974, the date of the completion of the last comprehensive plan. They also knew they wanted to engage the public—indeed their charge required it—but they feared the divisiveness and rancor of the typical public meeting. They learned about Grounded Visioning and eagerly incorporated it into their planning process.

Welcoming Format Encourages Citizen Participation

The committee's hope was to gain two outcomes from a series of interactive public sessions: a list of the enduring strengths of the town most worthy of preservation and a list of the challenges facing the town most worthy of future visioning. Since the committee was planning a long period of study and reflection, it was more interested in identifying challenges at the start than in actually engaging the public in visioning. So in this sense the classic Grounded Visioning session was revised. The core component that elicits dreams, hopes, and aspirations was replaced with an alternative exercise eliciting challenges and concerns for the future, in keeping with the needs of the sponsor. In other ways it followed the textbook pattern: flexible enough to accommodate as many people as showed up at a public meeting; fast enough to fit in a tight 90-minute window; easy enough to be facilitated by volunteers.

Table 17.1 shows the agenda that emerged to meet their needs.

Table 17.1
Grounded Visioning for Our Town: Agenda

Time (minutes)	Task
5	Opening
10	Do appreciative interviews
10	Share attractions
20	Share high point stories
40	Mind map future challenges and prioritize
5	Detail next steps

A "mind map" is a graphic portrayal of a series of interconnected issues and challenges.

Announcements went out all over town, with these enticing invitations and promises:

- "The Comprehensive Long Range Plan Committee needs your input! The future of Our Town is in your hands."
- "This information will be used to develop a long range plan for Our Town through the year 2020. This is your opportunity to make a difference in the course Our Town takes over the next twenty years."
- "Refreshments will be served and fun will be had by all."

Enduring Strengths of Our Town

Almost 100 people attended three sessions held in two different parts of town. Participants' attraction comments and high point stories helped articulate how Our Town is when it is at its very best. These insights coalesced into a list of the town's top 10 enduring strengths:

An Enduring Strength of Our Town is...

- The continuum of our history—political, ecological, intellectual, architectural, spiritual—and our connection to the past that we recreate year after year.
- Our respect and stewardship, and caring and activism, to protect our history, our lands, our buildings, and our water in the face of modern pressure.
- Our spirit and advantages as a small town, with a healthy mix of independent businesses, strong institutions, and residential, cultural, and open space resources.
- Our open town meeting and the supreme effort made by most citizens to listen, be respectful, and make a good decision, all with a sense of humor.
- Our schools and our commitment to education, and our kids who go forth in the world as positive and contributing people.
- The collective wisdom of multiple generations living together, made possible by our economic diversity and our caring for our elders.
- The abundance of diverse citizens willing and passionate to contribute to the town, working together as volunteers to make things happen.
- Our capacity as a town to take courageous initiative, to take on difficult issues, and to think and plan ahead.

- Our exceptional town government, the sense of safety in town, how willing town employees are to work with citizens.
- Our rural nature, open space, working farms, and conservation land trusts, giving us places to go where you're not crowded.

Critical Issues and Challenges Facing Our Town

Based on the participants' input in the mind mapping exercise, these critical issues emerged as most worthy of future visioning:

- Preserving what makes Our Town unique—its open space, historic lands and buildings, its healthy mix of businesses, housing, and institutions, in the face of increasing modern pressures.
- Maintaining open, civil, and respectful dialogue in an era of disputes over limited resources.
- Mitigating pressures from regional growth in the form of traffic, noise, cell towers, airport flights, and area shopping malls.
- Conserving and protecting wild life and open space in the face of increased public use of land resources.
- Mediating the tension of competing interests and priorities in the face of a perceived scarcity of fiscal resources and over reliance on property taxes.
- Mitigating pressures against economic and housing diversity from exploding land prices.
- Responding to increasing needs of the educational system for building upgrades and operating support.
- Upgrading the town's infrastructure in light of needs of police, fire, recreation, roads, schools, bridges, town buildings, septic systems, and telecommunications.
- Preserving local autonomy in the face of state and federal challenges to it, unfunded state and federal mandates, state influence on taxation policy, state-managed growth at nearby airport, and state planning mandates and local overrides.
- Responding to the effects of worldwide trends such as global population growth, global climate change, and global energy use patterns.

Helping Citizens Make Choices

Here's how the pilot process was described as experienced by a Comprehensive Long Range Planning Committee member, in a summary article, "Green Dots and Hot Spots—Planning [Our Town's] Future."[3] Remember that the typical focus on dreams, hopes, and aspirations was altered to instead focus on Our Town's emerging challenges and concerns.

"Now comes the fun part. You probably can't address all these challenges, so which are more important than others?" says Jay Vogt, with a knowing smile. "This is where you begin the process of prioritizing." Vogt's audience, comprising [Our Town's] Comprehensive Long Range Plan Committee (CLRPC) and a handful of other [Our Town] citizens, hesitate and begin to whisper among themselves. Open space or affordable housing? Lower taxes or improved services for seniors? Devote tax dollars to fight [airport] expansion or to protecting historic resources? And how do we pay for all this, anyway?

The summary article described the challenges of moving "from pie in the sky platitudes" to "a realistic, prioritized set of challenges to address." CLRPC members were surprised by the results:

Participants seem to have enjoyed the morning. "I was really surprised, and frankly delighted," said a CLRPC member...after the workshop completed. "We were all concerned that a 'public input workshop' could descend into a public rehashing of all that's wrong—assessments, [airports], schools, or whatever an individual's concerns are. Those concerns are all valid but repetition of known complaints is not particularly helpful. This workshop is fun, it's energetic, it's positive, and it forces you to choose the challenges where you want to devote the Town's resources."[4]

Getting beyond Platitudes

Because people work in pairs, Grounded Visioning helps participants get down to specifics. Even in a large group of people who may not know each other, it's possible to move beyond platitudes.

Throughout the morning, the series of exercises moves from the general to the specific, and includes a dynamic "Mind Map" exercise in which participants group challenges and issues facing Our Town by theme, like the branches on a tree. The process moves quickly, with no speaker holding the floor for more than a minute or so. Vogt scribbles hastily on a large easel as citizens call out ideas. "So we've identified a lot of strengths," Vogt says at one point. "What are the challenges? What are the forces most likely to have a detrimental impact on what we value here?"[5]

Planning committee members praised the opportunity to make choices within a positive context.

"We have high hopes for this process," enthuses [the committee chair]. "Nothing will be carved in marble when these workshops are complete. Citizens who might not be able to participate in these will have other chances to voice their views. But this is a good start. It gives us some guidance. Besides," he says with a smile, "it's a lot of fun."[6]

SERENDIPITY BRINGS COMMUNITY LEADERS TOGETHER; GROUNDED VISIONING CREATES ENGAGEMENT

The new governor had made civic engagement one of the central themes of his highly successful campaign. He had accepted the invitation of a respected community leadership development program to address its graduates and supporters on that very subject, and nearly 400 business and community leaders were expected to pack a hotel ballroom for the 45-minute speech. The organizers were thrilled. There was just one problem. It wouldn't be right to just "talk" about civic engagement. They wanted to "do" something about it too. They wanted to actually make civic engagement happen. But how? With 400 people who didn't know each other? From different communities? In less than 90 minutes?

The sponsors needed 20 of the 90 minutes before the speech to welcome people and recognize community leadership achievements. So just over an hour was left to make a difference in the lives of these 400 participants, and their communities. As with tackling all large challenges, the sponsors needed to break this down into smaller, more manageable pieces.

Sort by Common Interests to Find Common Ground

First I asked that the large group of 400 divide into 50 groups of eight seated at round tables. Easily done. Next, I assumed that people who shared common interests would, when asked to discover a way to work together, be more likely to find common ground more quickly.

How could people of similar interests gather at the same table? It so happens that this Community Leadership Program educates its aspiring leaders in about 10 topic areas, for example, education, health, and government. We assigned each of the 10 topics to five tables; small signs indicated which tables featured which topics. It was then a simple matter to ask incoming participants to sit at tables featuring a topic of personal interest to them.

Due to the extremely limited time, I needed to increase our chances that the key self-management leadership role to be played at each table work group would succeed. So I asked the organizers to do something I rarely do: to recruit hosts in advance for each table to facilitate the introductions of strangers and to moderate the brief table work group conversations. Typically the people who volunteer for this key role on the spot do just fine. By recruiting capable leaders in advance, I had more confidence that this would be the case.

Table 17.2 summarizes the agenda for this large meeting with broad goals.

Table 17.2
Community Engagement Forum: Agenda

Time (minutes)	Task
10	Explain task to large group
15	Share high point stories at tables about civic engagement
5	Identify common themes from high point stories at tables
15	Brainstorm civic engagement initiatives at tables that this group could do or support
15	Identify one or two actions on which this group could work together
10	Hear highlights from table work group reporters in large group

Other roles were not preassigned. As part of the explanation of the task, I asked people at each table to assume the self-management roles that typically assist in the table work group's success. The table work groups selected a time-keeper, recorder, reporter, and data manager.

Next, I asked participants to share a high point story about a time when they had been highly energized by a civic engagement challenge, ideally in the content area of their table's topic. People shared their stories, one at a time going around the circle, while introducing themselves as they went. It was then easy, having heard eight stories, for the table participants to identify common themes that emerged.

The 15-Minute Miracle

Here is where I really went "off-road." I asked the table groups to brainstorm ideas, in 15 minutes or less, for an actual civic engagement project that they could really undertake together, or at least one that was already underway, that they could in some way support. I had no real idea, having never done this before, whether a group of strangers could make this leap together. Then, I asked groups that had brainstormed a list of projects to actually pick one, in their last 15 minutes, and set a time to take real next steps.

It is probably best to hear what really happened in the words of an actual participant, who wrote up his experience.[7]

> First, they told their stories. Around the table, they were given two minutes each to say who they were and what had first drawn them to community service. One said John F. Kennedy had inspired him to join the Peace Corps. One volunteered to help a library fund-raising campaign. Another lost a friend to domestic violence and decided, in her memory, to help out at a shelter for battered women. One said residential growth was eating away at his hometown's rural beauty, so he volunteered for the open space committee. The stories came out at table after table, from one end of the [hotel] ballroom to the other. They were just the icebreakers, but they provided vital reference points.
>
>   The talk then turned to ideas. Our communities have all kinds of needs, and government can't fill them all. What could the people at each table do to make MetroWest a better place? The ideas flowed on to flip charts at every table:
>
> - Start a Web site for kids, sort of a MySpace MetroWest, so young people could connect with others in nearby towns.
> - Organize a family day to get people out to the region's art museums, historical places, parks, and libraries.
> - Clean up around area reservoirs—and partner with the [local] state college to get young volunteers.
> - Help immigrants connect with the community and aspire to the middle class by building up the [local] ESL (English as a Second Language) program.
> - Create an online database for organizations that welcome volunteers.

- Pull together leaders from [neighboring towns] to brainstorm opportunities for collaboration.
- Create a welcome packet for newcomers, with information about organizations, public safety, local government and volunteer opportunities.
- Organize, support, publicize and attend a Community Party scheduled [locally] November 17.

The ideas and the participants ran the gamut. The arts people connected with the schools people, the corporate types with the political types, the nonprofit folks with the young activists. Business cards and e-mail addresses were exchanged. Plans were made to get together again. And connections were made. The woman who had worked on the battered women's shelter said that the shelter was under new management, and that she had been left in charge of the bank balance. Her goal was to find a way to put that money back in the service of women in crisis. Across the table, two women who work with the [community] foundation were more than happy to help. The newspaper guy at the table—that would be me—offered to publicize whatever they came up with.

So it was at each of [50] tables: introductions, followed by inspiration, ideas and making connections. The excited buzz that filled the ballroom was the sound of civic engagement. Civic engagement is a newly fashionable phrase, but it's much more than a buzzword. It is the means by which communities are built and sustained. It is neighbors, needs and organizations coming together. A hundred years ago, when people didn't move around so much, when towns were smaller and families were larger, building and sustaining communities came naturally. Now it takes a special effort, and special institutions, like [Community Leadership Program], which hosted the "Engaging Conversations" breakfast at the [hotel].

Dialogue across Public, Private, and Nonprofit Sectors

Weeks later, the executive director enthused about the impact of these 70 minutes on her community:

We had high expectations for the Forum, but it went above and beyond anything we could have imagined. It was an amazing morning, and the feedback from attendees has been incredible. Even people I know who I thought might be cynical or bored by a "table activity" were thrilled by the conversations and the connections they made with people they might otherwise never get to know. I was in awe as hundreds of people in the same room were actively engaged in creating ideas to make the community a better place.

Forum attendees hatched dozens of civic initiatives across a wide range of community themes and made commitments to one another to go beyond just talk and take personal or group action.

The executive director continued:

Here's some feedback from the evaluations: 91% of the participants said the Forum was "excellent," and the most important part of the day for the greatest percentage of attendees was the civic engagement exercises. I have to tell you that after weeks since our "Engaging Conversations" Forum, not a day goes by that I don't meet one or more people who attended the event and have genuine praise for what went on in the room that morning. I've heard from several people that they are staying in touch with their table partners, and I am sure we will be seeing some terrific end results from many of the initiatives that developed around the tables.

The executive director noted that the forum brought people from across the public, private, and nonprofit sectors into meaningful dialogue and action: "The immediate results of the event were tremendous and we believe the long-term positive results will have a measurable impact in our communities."

NOTES

1. http://www.concordnet.org/pages/ConcordMA_Finance/appa.html (accessed May 28, 2008).

2. Ibid.

3. Excerpts from Jim Reynolds, "Green Dots and Hot Spots—Planning [Our Town's] Future," *The Concord Journal*, March 7, 2002. Reprinted with permission.

4. Ibid.

5. Ibid.

6. Ibid.

7. Excerpts from Rick Holmes, "Building Community One Idea at a Time," *The Daily News Tribune,* April 25, 2007; for more detail, see http://www.dailynewstribune.com/opinion/x1216748976. Reprinted with permission.

18

Organizations as Living Things

Leaders who invite participation create visions that live.

The significant problems we face cannot be solved at the same level of thinking we were at when we created them.

———Albert Einstein

The simple miracle of Grounded Visioning is that a large group of people—even strangers—can come together, perhaps for the first time, and share their innermost dreams, hopes, and aspirations. Through this private sharing, they quickly find surprisingly large and public areas of common ground with their companions. How is this remarkable thing possible?

ORGANIZATIONS ARE NOT MACHINES

In our industrial age, we frequently use mechanical metaphors for describing organizations. We "build" teams and "run" organizations. We call our techniques "tools" and our procedures "mechanisms." The ultimate compliment is when a great team works together "like a well-oiled machine." This notion of organizations as machines is deeply ingrained. It is well established in our language, so much so that we don't even notice it. You can even find it in the title of this book, *Recharge Your Team.*

Viewing organizations as machines means the success of any company must be limited to the capabilities of its "operating system," the leadership vision put forward by the "operator," that is, the CEO or the management team. When managers are unusually gifted or very lucky, this directive leadership from above can work well. But when the competitive environment is changing rapidly or when customers with new needs and demands are pushing the company into new markets, such top-down thinking can, in machine-speak, "gum up the works."

ORGANIZATIONS ARE LIVING SYSTEMS

But a new way of looking at organizations is emerging that models companies on living systems, not on machines.

Look at the way your body fights infection. Who is in charge of this highly successful effort? Certainly not the brain. It happens naturally through the innumerable interactions of autonomous cells. A natural order emerges when the conditions are right, even if no one is in charge.

Can organizations heal themselves like our bodies heal themselves? What if ailing companies, under attack from competitors, had the capacity to organize themselves to do exactly what was necessary to restore competitive integrity?

We can reject the machine-based view and suppose that an organization collectively possesses the intelligence of a living organism. The living metaphor suggests that a group of intelligent and independent employees collectively possesses a natural and inherent adaptability, like a body composed of vital, integrated cells. Consider:

- Employees are often closer to the customer and the learning edges than senior management.
- Employees may be the first to sense an attack and the fastest to be in position to repel it swiftly.

Leaders in many organizations are stepping back from relying solely on themselves as the source of competitive strategy, knowledge, and vision and are instead fostering environments in which competitive strategy and vision can emerge from their people. Let's call this approach "emergent strategy." Emergent strategy is not imposed, it is revealed. Christopher Meyer and Stan Davis define the biological concept of emergence as "the way unpredictable patterns arise from innumerable interactions between independent parts."[1] Emergence describes, for example, the way healthful patterns that support life in our body arise from the innumerable interactions of our autonomous yet interrelated cells.

The same challenges that bedevil us when we think of organizations as machines can enliven us when we think of them as living organisms.

GROUNDED VISIONS ARE ALIVE

Grounded Visioning is one way to engage the inherent, natural intelligence of people in organizations that function more like living organisms than machines:

- Grounded Visions emerge.
- Grounded Visions are shared.
- Grounded Visions create commitment.

Six Steps to a Grounded Vision

- Assemble your stakeholders
- Ignite the spark
- Share best practices
- Share your dreams
- Select the best
- Plan next steps

Grounded Visions Emerge

One tangible way we can shift our focus from the machine view of organizations to a living-systems view is to be receptive to opportunities where strategy wants to bubble up—where it wants to *emerge*. Grounded Visioning sets the conditions for the emergence of vision. Recall Meyer and Davis's formula for emergence: "unpredictable patterns arise from innumerable interactions between independent parts."

Figure 18.1
Grounded Visions emerge: Interactions among participants bring forth a positive envisioned future.

Illustration by Cindy Murphy.

In a large group process, in particular, each table work group functions as "independent parts" composed of employees, customers, suppliers, and anyone else who cares about what the organization does and how well it does it. No external facilitator or leader directs these conversations. They are independent and autonomous.

The work these groups do—through appreciative interviews and group tasks—fosters "innumerable interactions" among participants simultaneously in the session. Indeed, the four appreciative questions invoke a powerful vitality and surface life-giving forces in organizations. They bring forth a positive envisioned future and a sense of how the organization is when it is at its very best.

The physical building of these data points into an emergent whole—through affinity diagramming—completes the process in a way that no one individual controls. No one is really in charge. "Unpredictable patterns" literally arise from the interactions of the independent parts. Our cases show that, within four hours, a large group of wary strangers can find themselves so moved by these patterns—by their shared vision—that they will volunteer to implement it in large numbers.

New Role for Leaders

Grounded Visions do not come from leaders who believe it is their job, or perhaps their privilege, to set a vision and then call on others to share it. In such cases, commitment only happens if those beneath them agree, either willingly or through the intimidation of hierarchy.

Instead the new view of organizations as living systems tells us that an organization has an innate capacity within itself to organize itself toward what is best. The capacity is there, the common ground is there, the collective will to make it happen is already there. We just need to surface it. Shared vision already exists within our organization. We don't need to impose it; we just need to let it emerge.

Grounded Visioning is great news for leaders. It means there is an unseen, and often untapped, collective intelligence in their people that is deeper and more powerful than the intelligence of any single participant. To access it they must be willing to shift their focus from directing people in the right ways to convening them in the right ways.

A new role emerges for leaders who seek a shared vision with their people:

- The role of leaders shifts from imposing a vision to allowing one to be revealed.
- The role of leaders shifts from creating the vision to creating the conditions in which the vision can emerge.
- The role of leaders shifts from identifying problems to appreciating strengths.
- The role of leaders shifts from inspiring with a compelling vision to trusting that a compelling and inspiring vision wants to come forward—and will.

The community college president quoted at the end of Chapter 13 has led her institution in this way for more than 10 years and enjoyed phenomenal growth and national recognition as a result. Every three or four years she invites 250 external and internal stakeholders to come together for half a day to set goals for the college. She sets no constraints other than that the goals must fulfill the mission of the college. Every year she convenes 150 internal stakeholders for a day to create action plans to move the college toward those goals. She is absolutely committed to transformation, yet the shared vision of what that means, year to year, emerges from these stakeholders, in these dynamic sessions.

YOUR TEAM'S VISION: WAITING TO EMERGE

Grounded Visioning is a simple yet powerful tool to help a shared vision emerge from a large, diverse, and even conflicted set of stakeholders in very little time. Indeed, something transformational takes place. Something greater is achieved than can be found in the sum of all the individual parts.

It takes courage for many to move from a hierarchical, mechanistic view of organizations to an interconnected, biological view of organizations as living systems. It can be scary, and it goes against the grain for many. The old way is more comfortable, and much better known. The new way requires trust that a natural intelligence is present that may not yet have revealed itself. The new way requires attention to the environment to create conditions to call it forth. The new way seeks a vision of the future that is grounded in the realities of how the organization (or team or community) works when it is at its best.

It's not a blue-sky, anything goes, vision that may or may not be attained, but a grounded one, based on actual best practices. That vision lives within your team, company, organization, or community, waiting to emerge, waiting for you to help bring it forth, again and again.

NOTE

1. Christopher Meyer and Stan Davis, *It's Alive: The Coming Convergence of Information, Biology, and Business* (New York: Crown Business, 2003).

APPENDICES

Planning Documents, Sample Agendas, Sample Handouts for Large Groups, and Follow-up and Evaluation

Meeting Room Specifications

Room
- The room should be large enough to comfortably accommodate round tables for seating participants.
- The room must have at least one wall for posting brown kraft paper—ceiling to floor is ideal. Two or three walls are better. We want to be able to post newsprint on the walls for the entire meeting. Art work should be removed from walls if possible. If no suitable work surfaces exist on walls, foam core sheets must be introduced.
- The room or its entrance should include space for registration tables.
- The environment should be comfortable both inside and out to enable participants to rejuvenate and refresh themselves during the time together.

Tables
- Each participant table should be able to comfortably sit eight or nine persons and should be round with comfortable chairs.
- The front of the room should include a small table for the facilitators and two easels.
- The back of the room should include a small table for conference staff and recorders.
- Each table should have one easel and one flip chart. These can be set to the side of the room at the start of each day until needed, to improve sight lines.
- Each table should be marked with a number or color code. Each should be set with water, markers, masking tape, adhesive notes, adhesive dots, and decorations as appropriate.

Registration
- The registration table should include participant workbooks, name badges, logistics information.
- Participant workbooks may contain a schedule, a participant list, table assignments, worksheets, handouts, note paper, pens.

Sound System
- A sound system and four microphones are needed: two wireless mikes for the facilitators and two cordless microphones that can be passed from table to table.

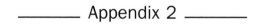

Appendix 2

Materials and Equipment List

Before the Meeting

- Confirmation letter sent to participants prior to conference

In the Room

- Workbooks: one per participant
- Table assignments: typically on name tags
- Name tags: one for each participant (typically with table assignments)
- Round tables: one per work group
- Six-foot table: set in the front of room for facilitators
- Amplification system: one wireless mike for each facilitator, plus at least two cordless mikes for tables to use in making small group reports
- Refreshments: healthy, please
- Meals: healthy, please
- Trash receptacles: at least one at the front and one at the back of the room
- Kraft paper: brown paper sheets creating a Vision Wall about 8' by 24'
- Foam core sheets: sheets of foam core, 3/16" wide, and 4 feet by 8 feet, to create light yet rigid work surfaces, if none other exists

At the Tables

- Name tents/table stands: one per table, coded by number
- Flip charts and easel: one per table, plus two for the facilitators
- Pads and pencils: one per participant
- Colored dots: available at each table
- 3' × 5' adhesive notes: several 100-sheet pads per table, one color per table
- Water-based markers: one set per table, plus one set for each facilitator
- Masking tape: one roll per table plus one roll for facilitators
- 3" adding machine paper roll: one per table
- Scissors: one per table
- Bottle of bubble-making liquid with wand: one per table
- Camera: one disposable camera per table (optional)
- Table decorations: simple, inexpensive, creative, just for fun (optional)

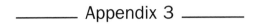

Appendix 3

Sample Small Group Agenda

PROPOSED AGENDA

Grounded Visioning for Our Town's Downtown

Overall Purpose

Create shared vision for the future of Our Town's downtown

Desired Outcomes

- Positive connection and commitment to the work of Downtown Center Associates
- List of improvement goals (and priorities) for downtown Our Town
- Clarity about next steps

Proposed Agenda

Start time	Minutes	Task
6:00	15	Welcome: Outcomes, agenda, roles, rules
6:15	5	Explain task
6:20	20	Appreciative interviewing in pairs (10 minutes each): attractions, high points, dreams, and aspirations
6:40	10	Share some highlights of what attracted folks to Our Town's downtown and keeps them
6:50	10	Share a few stories of high points in people's experience of Our Town
7:00	30	Post dreams and aspirations; build clusters and like ideas
7:30	15	Set priorities using multi-voting; share reactions briefly
7:45	15	Review next steps: • Describe upcoming public meetings • Describe next steps for work groups • Describe preparations for further planning sessions
8:00		Adjourn

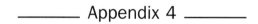

Appendix 4

Sample Large Group Agenda

PROPOSED AGENDA

Grounded Visioning for Our Organization

Overall Purpose

Define a shared vision and direction for Our Organization

Desired Outcomes

- Share what's best about Our Organization in a fun and positive way
- Set key goals for Our Organization's desired achievements in the next two to three years
- Set up goal teams for action planning as part of a strategic plan

Proposed Agenda

Start time	Minutes	Task	Handouts/ Worksheets
12:00	60	Gathering: Brown bag lunch	
Welcome			
1:00	8	Share hopes for the afternoon; ask stakeholders to stand by groups	
	7	Clarify outcomes, agenda, roles, rules	Appendices 5 and 6

High Points about Our Organization

1:15	5	Explain five roles, ask people to choose roles, explain task	Appendices 7 and 8
	20	At tables, people introduce themselves and share stories	Appendix 8
	5	Explain task: List common themes	Appendix 9
	20	Tables identify common themes and list them, develop belief statements	Appendix 9
	15	Reporters share themes with the large group	
	15	Break	

Shared Vision for Our Organization

2:35	5	Explain task: Work in pairs to identify dreams	Appendix 10
	10	In pairs, people write down their dreams	Appendix 10
	5	Explain tasks: Cluster goals and choose the best	Appendix 11
	25	Tables cluster goals and choose the best	Appendix 11
	30	Dreams posted, clustered, and titled on the Vision Wall	
	15	Set priorities: explain multi-voting, vote, and tally the results	

Next Steps

4:05	10	Explain next steps and ask for volunteers	Appendices 12 and 13
	15	Invite participants to express appreciations and complete evaluation form	Appendix 14
4:30		Adjourn	

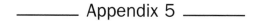 **Appendix 5** ————

Sample Summary Agenda

AGENDA

Grounded Visioning for Our Organization

Overall Purpose

Define a shared vision and direction for Our Organization

Desired Outcomes

- Share what's best about Our Organization in a fun and positive way
- Set key goals for Our Organization's desired achievements in the next two to three years
- Set up goal teams for action planning as part of a strategic plan

Agenda

Optional brown bag lunch and tour at noon
Opening at 1 P.M.
Welcome
First group task: Share high point stories about Our Organization
Break
Second group task: Create shared vision for Our Organization's desired achievements in next two to three years
Closing: Next steps/action plans
Adjourn no later than 5 P.M.

Appendix 6

Roles and Ground Rules

Roles
Consultants:

- Set time and tasks
- Facilitate large group discussions
- Keep purpose front and center
- Assist in follow-through

Participants:

- Provide information and make meaning
- Manage own small groups
- Develop vision and commit to it
- Engage in actions to make vision real

Ground Rules

- Remember: All ideas are valid
- Listen to understand, not judge
- Acknowledge differences, but don't "work" them
- Write everything on flip charts
- Observe time frames for tasks
- Seek common ground and joint action
- Have fun while getting lots done!

———— Appendix 7 ————

How Participants Help Facilitate

ROLES FOR SMALL GROUP DISCUSSIONS

Each small group manages its own discussion, data, time, and reports. Leadership roles can be rotated. Divide up the work as you wish.

- **Facilitator:** Assures that each person who wants to speak is heard within time available. Keeps group on track to finish on time.
- **Timekeeper:** Keeps group aware of time left. Monitors report-outs and signals time remaining to person talking.
- **Recorder:** Writes group's output legibly on flip charts, using each speaker's words. Asks people to restate long ideas briefly.
- **Reporter:** Delivers report to large group in time allotted.
- **Data manager:** Labels each record of the group's output. Takes output to meeting organizers responsible for collecting data.

Everyone can help the facilitator:

- Ensure that a climate of mutual and respectful listening exists at the table.
- Create an environment where people feel free both to strongly assert their points of view and to hold those same views open to inquiry.
- Hear from everyone, yet without anyone dominating the conversation.
- Support the group in reaching agreement on priorities as required by tasks, recognizing everyone has to show flexibility in the limited time allowed.
- Move the group from one task to another so as to accomplish the whole task in the time allowed.
- Give corrective feedback when some behavior is obviously keeping the group from accomplishing their tasks and fulfilling their potential.

——— Appendix 8 ———

High Points: Stories

HIGH POINTS ABOUT OUR ORGANIZATION

WORKSHEET
TIMEKEEPER: YOU HAVE 20 MINUTES FOR THIS TASK

Purpose

- Introduce yourselves to fellow stakeholders at your table.
- Help us connect with what works about Our Organization.

Tasks

- Decide on leadership roles for your group (Appendix 7).
- **Facilitator:** Make sure that each person shares his or her name and a story in *no more than 2 minutes.* Take no more than 20 minutes for all your introductions and stories.
- **Timekeepers:** Alert speakers when their time is up.
- **Participants:** Share your name and a story of a high point in your experience of Our Organization—a time when you felt most engaged, proud, connected, inspired...

High Points: Themes

WHAT HIGH POINTS SAY ABOUT OUR ORGANIZATION

WORKSHEET
TIMEKEEPER: YOU HAVE 20 MINUTES FOR THIS TASK

- **Facilitator:** Take *10 minutes* and help the group identify *common themes* in the stories you've just heard. Ask: "What are the common themes in our stories?"
- **Recorder:** Write down the common themes identified by participants on the flip chart.

- **Facilitator:** Take another *10 minutes* and develop *one or two statements of belief*—one or two things your group believes about how Our Organization is when it is at its best, based on the common themes everyone has shared. Ask the group to complete the sentence, *"When Our Organization is at its best, we..."*
- **Recorder:** Write out the one or two beliefs large and legibly.

- **Reporter:** Present your one or two belief statements as directed by the facilitators.
- **Data manager:** Post the theme posters and the belief posters as directed by the facilitators.

Appendix 10

Dreams: Interviewing

OUR DREAMS, HOPES, AND ASPIRATIONS FOR WHAT OUR ORGANIZATION
CAN ACHIEVE

WORKSHEET

PARTICIPANTS: YOU HAVE 10 MINUTES FOR THIS TASK

Purpose

- Share our dreams, hopes, and aspirations for what Our Organization can achieve in the next two to three years.
- Develop a shared vision of what Our Organization can achieve in the next two to three years.
- Set priorities among the great things Our Organization can achieve in the next two to three years.

Tasks

- Choose a partner for an activity in pairs.
- Make sure you have a few adhesive notes and something to write with.
- Ask your partner to imagine a positive future for Our Organization, and then to share two or three dreams, hopes, and aspirations for what it can achieve, say in two to three years' time.
- Record your partner's comments, one idea per note.
- Switch roles and repeat.
- Take no more than *five minutes* for each of you.

Dreams: Posting

SHARE DREAMS, HOPES, AND ASPIRATIONS

WORKSHEET
TIMEKEEPER: YOU HAVE 25 MINUTES FOR THESE TASKS

- Decide on leadership roles for your group (Appendix 7).

- **Facilitator:** Ask the first person to read aloud and post his or her three notes on your flip chart. Ask the second person to read aloud and post his or her three notes. When one of the ideas is new, make sure it is posted apart from the other ideas. When one of the ideas is similar to a previously posted idea, make sure it is posted physically right beside the similar idea, thus building a cluster of like ideas. Continue until everyone's ideas are posted and all similar ideas are posted together.
- **Recorder:** Help with posting and sorting of notes.

- **Facilitator:** Briefly review each idea in a cluster of ideas and help the group pick one idea that best captures the essence of all the notes in that grouping. Ask: "Which note best captures the essence of this group of notes?" Make that the "header."
- **Recorder:** Help post the headers at the top of their groupings.

- **Facilitator:** Help the group identify two or three main goals, end results, or desired outcomes that represent the best thinking of the table. Ask: "Of all these good ideas, which two or three represent our best thinking?" Remember: Don't focus on how you would make this idea come about—leave that for the goal teams. Focus on what you want to see, have, or achieve.
- **Recorder:** Write the main goals out largely and legibly on special mini-posters.

- **Reporter:** Post the mini-posters as directed by the facilitators.
- **Data manager:** Post the notes posters as directed by the facilitators.

- **Timekeeper:** Allow no more than 25 *minutes* for these tasks.

Planning Template:
Focus on Quarterly Milestones

GOAL TEAM ACTION PLANNING TEMPLATE

Goal	
One Year Measurable Results	
Quarter 1 Actions	
Quarter 1 Milestones	
Quarter 2 Actions	
Quarter 2 Milestones	
Quarter 3 Actions	
Quarter 3 Milestones	
Quarter 4 Actions	
Quarter 4 Milestones	

Volunteer Sign-Up Sheet

VOLUNTEER SIGN-UP

I'm willing to help!

Last name _____
First name _____
Street address _____
Phone (day) _____
Phone (eve) _____
E-mail (please print clearly) _____

Check all that apply!
- I want to work with a goal team.
  • First choice: _____
  • Second choice: _____
- I want to co-lead a goal team.
- I want to review drafts of a goal team (by e-mail).
  • First choice: _____
  • Second choice: _____
- I want to help raise funds.

Thank you very much!

Evaluation Form

EVALUATION

What were the most significant outcomes of this day for you?

On a scale of 1 to 10, how confident are you that we will achieve the results we defined today?

Not a snowball's chance	1	2	3	4	5	6	7	8	9	10	Watch our dust!

Why did you mark it as high as you did?

What do we need to do from here to maintain our momentum?

Thank you!

Index

About the Author

JAY W. VOGT is an organizational and human development consultant who founded Peoplesworth, a consultancy, in 1982. Clients include Nortel Networks, Stonyfield Farm, Harvard University, the Massachusetts Audubon Society, and many other mission-driven organizations.